LION RAMPANT

Robert Woollcombe was born in 1922 in London and was educated at Marlborough College. His family's association with the King's Own Scottish Borderers spanned three generations: his uncle was killed in action with the KOSB in France in 1914; his grandfather was colonel of the regiment and commanded IV Army Corps, which bore the brunt of the Battle of Cambrai in 1917; and Robert himself enlisted in the 60th Rifles in 1941 and was commissioned into the 6th Battalion in 1942, with which he served in north-west Europe. He served with the 2nd KOSB in India from 1945 to '46. Later, he lived in West Sussex and had two daughters and a son. Robert Woollcombe died in 1996.

In August 2006 the King's Own Scottish Borderers merged with the Royal Scots Battalion to become the Royal Scots Borderers, 1st Battalion, the Royal Regiment of Scotland (1 SCOTS).

LION RAMPANT

ROBERT WOOLLCOMBE

'O Lord judge between us and
our enemies, and if it be Thy will,
grant us the victory'
Church of Scotland field prayer

BLACK & WHITE PUBLISHING

First published 1955
This edition published 2014
by Black & White Publishing Ltd
29 Ocean Drive
Edinburgh EH6 6JL

ISBN 978 1 84502 781 0

A CIP catalogue record for this book is available
from the British Library.

Typeset by RefineCatch Ltd, Bungay

Printed and bound by Grafica Veneta S.p.A. Italy

AUTHOR'S NOTE

THE British like best to think back on themselves in honourable adversity; but this is a tale of Victory.

In checking certain details of background I have made grateful use of the *History of the 15th Scottish Division*, by Lieutenant-General H. G. Martin, C.B., D.S.O., O.B.E., and of the war accounts of the brigade and battalion with which I served—*From Normandy to the Baltic; the Story of the 44th Lowland Brigade*, by Ian M. Robertson; and *The 6th (Border) Battalion: the King's Own Scottish Borderers: 1939-1945*, by J. R. P. Baggaley, M.C.

I am grateful also to the late Field-Marshal Viscount Montgomery of Alamein and Messrs Hutchinson & Co. Ltd. for permission to reprint a passage from *Normandy to the Baltic* (1947); to Her Majesty's Stationery Office for permission to quote a sentence from the Report of the Supreme Commander to the Combined Chiefs of Staff on the Operations in Europe of the Allied Expeditionary Force 1944-45; and to the *Illustrated London News* for permission to quote an extract from their issue of 17th March 1945.

CONTENTS

PROLOGUE

IT was New Year's Eve, 1943-44. The sergeants were holding a Guest Night in their Mess beyond the roundabout in a Yorkshire village on the Great North Road, and the guests were the officers. It was our last normal station in England.

And there was the Regimental Sergeant-Major, that New Year's Eve, standing on a table with the Great North Road outside, delivering himself of a genial number with "bags o' patter." . . . And I remember, shortly before midnight, talking to Colour-Sergeant Macbain, the oldest soldier in "A" Company. He had just given me another beer and had one himself, and his face was at its reddest, when slowly it dawned on me that nothing he was saying made the slightest sense whatever. He looked as annoyed as he always did—he might have been making out a ration indent. But in his own way, Colour-Sergeant Macbain was comfortably, unnervingly intoxicated.

There were the rest of them from "A" Company: big "Tam" MacEwan, my platoon sergeant, among them, with my two fellow platoon commanders. Alastair, a year younger than I, was 8 Platoon. For his age, which was twenty, he was remarkably advanced where the opposite sex were concerned, and he always amazed me. Danny, a much older man but the junior subaltern, was 9 Platoon. Formerly a Territorial Colour-Sergeant, Danny was very dark and had a crackled voice heavily coated with the accent of Hawick. . . . And a little apart was the Company Sergeant-Major, with Gavin, our Company Commander.

Our sergeant-major had two exteriors: Fierce, and Baffled. Too much paper work baffled him, and once in a

9

boxing tournament he had slaughtered his opponent, an unfortunate young private, practically by sheer force of rank and presence, with hardly a blow being struck.

Gavin and Duncan were his only masters. Gavin with the somewhat rugged, pleasant features and the lazy wit; a peacetime soldier on his imperturbable way through the war. And Duncan, Gavin's second-in-command. The sweeping, highly strung, noisy, restless, blond big figure of Duncan. For a long time, by wartime reckoning, the "A" Company officers had been Duncan, myself and a wholehearted schoolboy we called Victor Sylvest, who died in a motorcycle smash. Duncan, a captain, had commanded—and one felt he still regarded the Company as his by right.

And then it was midnight. There was some singing and shouting.

"Well, Sergeant-Major. . . . Well, Woolbags. . . ." said Gavin, turning to the sergeant-major and myself in that deliberate way of his. "We're going to go through a hell of a battle this year, together."

"Yes, sir. A hell of a battle," agreed the sergeant-major, brisk and emphatic, rising to the moment. The more unpleasant a thing was likely to be, the more brisk and emphatic he invariably became. . . . And we all shook hands.

THE SUMMER

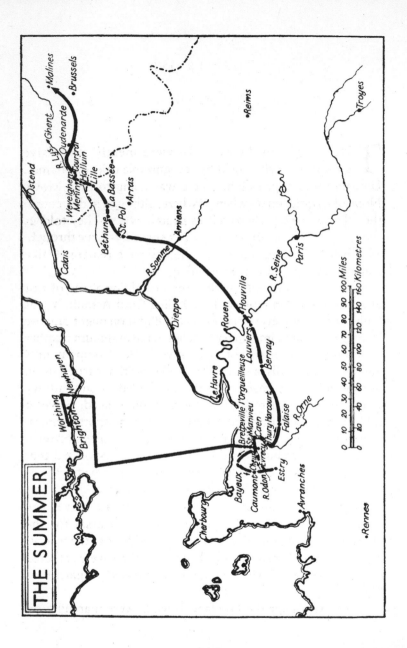

THE SUMMER

Malines
Brussels
Ghent
Oudenarde
R. Lys
Courtrai
Wevelghem
Menin
Halluin
Lille
La Bassée
Arras
St. Pol
Amiens
Reims
Troyes
Ostend
Béthune
Calais
R. Somme
R. Seine
Paris
Dieppe
Rouen
Louviers
Houville
R. Odon
Le Havre
Bernay
Cherbourg
Bayeux
Caumont
Briquessard
Bretteville l'Orgueilleuse
St. Manvieu
Caen
Tilly
Fontenay Harcourt
Estry
Falaise
R. Orne
Avranches
Worthing
Newhaven
Brighton
Rennes

0 10 20 30 40 50 60 70 80 90 100 Miles
0 20 40 60 80 100 120 140 160 Kilometres

CHAPTER ONE

PARADE

THE early months of 1944 were merely successive groups of weeks called by recognizable calendar names. Unreality was approaching: there was going to be a Move. None of us quite knew when or where, although in due course the villagers were able to tell us exactly when. They told us about a week before the secret movement orders came through. Meanwhile the old names on the calendar remained, like conventional signs on a strange map.

Soon there was built within the crumbling walls of our grounds a wooden replica of a Landing Craft Assault. It was built in order that every platoon in the Battalion might practise leaping off it on to imaginary beaches in the minimum number of seconds. And there it stood, between "A" Company huts and the dining-halls, a sort of Trojan Horse that carried us on our journeys over imaginary seas and landed us on shadowy coastlines somewhere beyond the unreality ahead; while at B.H.Q. the large form of Bob Wilson, motor transport technical sergeant, was bent with massive thoroughness, day by day, to the task of ensuring everything the Battalion possessed that moved on wheels could be driven through salt water for as long as the driver kept his neck above the surface.

Then, fast upon us, came the end of all leave, the censorship of mail, and a Brigade dress-rehearsal for the Divisional Commander's inspection and address to the troops. This last was exhaustive, and when two or three were gathered together over a NAAFI tea-counter was frankly regarded as "bull".

A few days later the Lowland Brigade were marching on

parade in a pleasant park to the familiar lilt of "Pibroch of Donhuil Dhu"—the gathering of the clans. Until an unreasonable hour the night before the atmosphere in billets had been thick with oaths and blanco. Never had quite such intensive "bull" been demanded, but the outraged Jock consoled himself with the reflection that it was "their last blanking chance".

The Brigade were to be drawn up in three sides of a square. The "Royals"—First of Foot—forming the right-flank battalion, the "Fusiliers" the centre battalion, with the massed pipes and drums in the rear of them, and we the left-flank battalion. In the centre of the square stood a jeep, and upon its bonnet, on a stand, was a microphone. After the inspection, ranks were to be broken and all were to gather round this vehicle and listen to the address. Facing the open side of the square across a small road that led to the parade-ground rose a whitewashed flagstaff, with the Brigade pennant crowning the proceedings at the top.

Suddenly, when the battalions were marching on to the parade, a rumour had issued out of the ground and was among us. Suddenly it was not the Divisional Commander after all who was going to inspect. Rapidly the word spread round, and as soon as the parade was drawn up the Brigadier reached for the microphone on the jeep and made an announcement. The rumour was confirmed. There was a stir.

The time for the expected arrival came and went. Half an hour passed. It was a crisp, sunny March afternoon with a scent of spring behind it, and everything was very still. The assembled ranks in bonnets, tam o' shanters, with their gleaming cap-badges and clean, sharply pressed and sun-splashed battle-dresses, waited. Some curious, some cynical, others still muttering about "bull" or a coarser word.

At length there came into view down the road out of the surrounding trees a lone despatch rider wearing vast driving-gauntlets blancoed a dazzling white, and belt to match. From his handlebars flew the large black-and-white check flag heralding the arrival of a Very Important Person. A short distance behind him came two more outriders, abreast, and then, at a discreet interval, there followed a large black car flying the Union Jack. Behind this there came the Divisional Commander's car, another car flying the Corps Commander's flag, then a carload of pressmen and cameramen, peculiarly out of place, and finally a jeep full of huge, immaculate Military Police. At a sedate pace the small convoy crunched to the flagstaff and stopped. Solitary in the silence came the Brigadier's voice calling the Brigade to attention as car doors slammed. Then the slope arms and a pause of deepest silence, and then the high, lone voice of the Brigadier again. . . . "General Salute Pre-sent Arms!" . . . Three measured movements from three thousand men, and to set the seal on it, the right hand of every officer snapping to his balmoral on the last movement of the rifles. All at once the pipes and drums broke into the first four bars of "Scotland the Brave", breaking off on the split second at a final thump from the big drums that cast the parade back with a jolt into a deep silence. Then the order arms, and at last the relief of the stand-at-ease, at which three thousand faces switch like another drill movement to the one direction. . . . Yes! Good heavens. There he was. Precisely as if he had stepped from the *Illustrated London News*. Behind him clustered his entourage, which for some reason included a Bishop. He was talking to the Brigadier, whose tubby figure, compact and concentrated as a bull terrier, was standing frantically to attention. Cameramen darted to and fro.

While the Brigade Staff were being introduced, A.D.C.s hurried across to bid battalion commanders that their men be divided, halfway down the files, and the front half faced about. This created a lane some two or three yards wide through all three sides of the square, down which he could walk, with the troops facing him on either side. Word was then given that ranks could be broken as he passed so that every man should have "a really good look" at him. This, it appeared, was most important. After that, no further orders were given and the troops remained standing easy, and with this strange blend of the informal and the electric, the inspection started.

It was hardly an inspection. It was a one-man progress. With his hands clasped behind him and well ahead of his entourage he slowly walked through the midst of the Lowland Brigade. For he was there to be seen. And see him they should: should know exactly what he looks like and who he is. They should absorb him. . . . And so they did. They forgot themselves, and struggled to catch sight of him. . . . Nor was this a man receiving his due, come to be acknowledged. But a man come, in some way, to know them. To every hundred pairs of eyes there were his to pierce back—they were the most arresting feature of him, the eyes. They dominated. Piercing grey eyes with a touch of blue that fairly bored into the rough kaleidoscopic crush of faces to both sides, leaving an impression of shrewd cold clarity that is not easily forgotten. With the eyes and the lean beaky face, and the tense spare figure, he seemed to be willing some part of himself into these, his unknown soldiers.

Through it all was the silence. A silence that lifted and tilted with the drowsy gay grief of the "Skye Boat Song" in slow march beat from the massed pipe bands of the three battalions, and the slow, punctuating roll of the drums. The silence accompanying him. The soldiers struggling to catch their glimpse, in silence, and his vivid, silent appraisal of them. An utter silence that added to the impressiveness of the hour something that has gone forever. There was a Biblical quality in its simplicity and note of faith. Aptly, here was the man who believed in the Lord, Mighty in Battle, and who took as his text the cry, "Let God arise, and let His enemies be scattered."

Afterwards, the address from the jeep.

Ranks were duly broken and a mob surged forward. The anxious voice of the Brigadier was heard above the multitude "Don't rush!—Don't rush!"—but went unheeded. And they settled themselves around the jeep at his feet. Standing at his ease at the microphone, he spoke: . . . . In 1940 was pushed back into the sea. . . . Didn't like it. . . . But a lot has happened since then. . . . Alamein. . . . Tripoli. . . . Tunis . . . . Enemy pushed back into sea. . . . Four hundred miles up Italy. . . . Some people say the Italian campaign slow—four hundred miles in four months fast enough for him! . . . R.A.F. now blasting West Wall to pieces. . . . Then we go over to mop up what's left. . . . Simple—quite simple! . . . All that's needed is confidence. . . . Must have our confidence. . . . Must have confidence in us. . . . Confidence. . . . Quite simple. . . .

The Brigadier called for three cheers, and they were given with a will. They may not have sounded the especial note of affection—"and another for luck!" that sped Winston Churchill, hunched and barely recovered from his illness, from the same parade-ground a week later. These were simply the cheers of soldiers for their Commander on the eve of a battle from which there was "nae turning back." These contained a tremendous note of relief. Relief and a kind of fervour. . . . We had the confidence! He had inspired it.

There followed a final glimpse of the vital figure walking back to the black car. . . . The Bishop taking his hat off high. . . . Turning for a last jaunty wave of the hand. . . . Then the cars crept off. The Brigade returned, refreshed, to billets.

The memory remains of the moment he appeared at the top of our flank, and Colonel Ben going forward to meet him to escort him through the Battalion. His slow approach down the lane. Your gaze takes in the highly polished, thick-soled brown shoes; travels upwards over buff-coloured canvas trousers; battle-dress blouse with a startling number of medal ribbons; to the face, bronzed and lined and older than you had imagined; over the deep lines formed on either side of a fiercely willed mouth; the thin, stern lips and scanty greying hair at the temples. And then the beret—with the two badges giving the brief ludicrous illusion of seeing double. For a disconcerting, unwavering second those amazing eyes penetrate straight into you at a range of three feet. In the same instant he has asked the Colonel a question—

"What's the average age of your battalion?"

"Twenty-five, sir"—promptly.

"Twenty-five? A good age, twenty-five. . . ." The tones were keen edged and very alert. As thin and wiry as the man. They repeated the age musingly. . . .

CHAPTER TWO

THE MOVE

BY April we knew the Move had begun. At first it was the Fire Services and St John's ambulances, string after string of them travelling through the village down the Great North Road. Everlasting assortments of ambulances, pumps, trailers and vans, whose crews apathetically chewed sandwiches as they bumped along or lounged by the roadside at halts, with crash-helmeted motorcyclists, their work cut out, shepherding them down the country. The scarcely spectacular harbingers of a greater exodus. . . . Then, the roads clear, came the steady high whine of Fordson engines, the whirr of solid thick tyres spinning through the village, and the "swoosh-swoosh" of vehicle displacement past the windows as the long mud-green columns rolled southwards. Hour upon hour, all day, every day, and into the night, they rumbled through and shook our ceilings. Emblazoned on every passing mudguard a clear white spearhead on a bright splash of red—the sign of Assault Corps.

Then it was our turn. Our transport joined the flowing arteries of road traffic. The marching personnel entrained at the railway station. In clusters about the pavements, at corners and in shop doorways the villagers collected to wave farewell.

A special train carried us south. Everywhere through London it was the same greeting; on walls and the backs of great high tenements overlooking the railway, painted in large, bold white lettering:

GOOD LUCK BOYS!

—while people waved from crowded back windows and in

groups along the embankment, and small boys ran shouting beside the track. . . . In a compartment full of subalterns Alastair and wee Fergie had a pocket edition of Burns open between them, and vociferously read it aloud together through the Sassenach capital:

> When chapman billies leave the street,
> And drouthy neibors neibors meet—

and they were away with Tam o' Shanter. Fergie, a tiny irrepressible man, formerly a sergeant-major in the "Royals". There was no alternative but to heed them:

> We think na on the lang Scots miles,
> The mosses, waters, slaps, and stiles,
> That lie between us and our hame,
> Whare sits our sulky, sullen dame,
> Gathering her brows like gathering storm,
> Nursing her wrath to keep it warm. . . .

Alastair tall and fair, Fergie dark and so small, and years apart. But both had that very Scots leanness, and both came from Penicuik:

> She tauld thee weel thou was a skellum,
> A bletherin', blusterin', drunken blellum—

this from Fergie, feelingly. He was the married one. Then wholeheartedly we had the lines to a mouse, and London was left behind:

> Wee sleekit, cow'rin', tim'rous beastie,
> O what a panic's in thy breastie!
> Thou need na start awa sae hasty,
>   Wi' bickerin' brattle!
> I wad be laith to rin an' chase thee,
>   Wi' murd'rin' pattle! . . .

At length, in darkness and an air-raid alert, the train drew in to Worthing, on the coast. The Divisional Concentration Area.

The entire Brigade were billeted in empty requisitioned boarding-houses along a mile stretch of sea front—the "Front Line", as Private Pratt, the one soldier in 7 Platoon who hailed from Sussex, called it with native pride. Across in Brighton were the tanks of the Guards Armoured Division, one of the two armoured divisions that together with us formed the Corps of the White Knight of Sir Richard O'Connor. Daily with the fair weather the bombers thundered out over the coast towards France, sparkling packs, silver in the sun. The soldiers below were kept fit and in trim. April turned to May, and May wore on. There was sunshine and showers, and days when the sea was choppy. But the predominant memory is of the sunshine, and marching up to the Downs, and the blue skies with the bombers going over the coast in the mornings. . . . Other memories jumble behind one another. The Company marching through West Sussex on a kind of round tour, bivouacking out, and returning at evening in the last glimmers of double summertime from country pubs and darts, to groundsheets and blankets in some wood among the cries of owls, and stillness. Having group photographs taken early one morning on the sea front, instead of P.T., and the sun slanting across all the cap-badges. A gloomy lecture in the forlorn pier pavilion by the Doctor, who was not designed to give lectures, on First Aid. Being trooped into the Odeon for a special showing of the film *Desert Victory*. Gaps cleared through the mines on the beach, and going down to bathe, and low tide and sands and some Jock in "C" Company being chased by his friends brandishing crabs. Night patrols on the golf-course, and stopping some startled car-driver for a lift home with our faces blackened with burnt cork. . . . and always marching. Marching by the sea and through the villages over the South Downs; and that signature tune of my own 7 Platoon. Their marching-song. Whose words I could

21

never remember except the chorus that ended with enormous verve:

> Roll me o—ver in the clo—ver,
> Roll me over lay me down and do it again.

All was well if they sang. . . . but increasingly they looked up, when one went round billets, to ask with a kind of hope, "When do you think it will be, sir?" It was the waiting that was trying. The waiting would have maddened had we not been kept busy.

Towards the end of the month an inter-brigade sports meeting took place in the Hove Greyhound Stadium. Most of the Division turned up, and many of the local population. The most entertaining event was an impromptu Senior Officers race. Our Brigadier, despite his well-stocked figure, was nimble enough, and at the pistol he fairly twinkled down the course, hardly touching the ground. But for all his efforts he was remorselessly overhauled by a galloping vision in a kilt, rapidly approaching from a short distance in rear. This was the Brigadier of one of the Highland brigades, who later took command of the Division and was dubbed by the press "the tallest general in the British Army." He was, in fact, six feet seven. Nature had concentrated everything upon a sheer upward thrust, so that he was all bone, angles and vast knees. He had fine silvering hair, a magnificent face, a deep gruff voice to match, and normally strode about with an outsize cromach, itself the height of ordinary men. In his great kilt of a Cameron Highlander he was awesome. For an unforgettable second the two were neck-and-neck, then in a whirl of knees he went ahead of our own twinkling little Brigadier like an inspired giraffe, to resounding cheers of encouragement from his soldiery.

After the final event the Divisional Commander, who was to be wounded in Normandy, said a few words from the grandstand. The General had fought in North Africa and Sicily. He had a vibrant quality. Everything about him seemed crisp and enlivening. He said something suitable to the occasion, and followed with something about "this wonderful Division of ours" in a voice that rang. . . . Then the massed pipe bands marched into the stadium to beat Retreat. The place was now packed.

These rare displays of the entire Divisional pipes and drums expressed the corporate spirit of the 15th Scottish Division. Represented here were the intermingled tartans of almost every infantry regiment of Scotland. Even the Divisional Artillery contributed a band to that moving maze, marching and countermarching, of kilts and sporrans and the trews of the drummers. Upwards of a hundred pipers there, and over fifty drums. The great cry of the pipes ascending, weaving its spell. In front, a solid row of pipe-majors. And in front of all, the drum-major—who came from our own battalion. We were always rather proud of this, and at the head of all his bands he was superb. His finest moment was perhaps when the great wide-flung circle of pipers was formed, slipping on the beat of ten big drums and all the tenors from quick march to reel, from reel to strathspey, and our drum-major supreme in the centre, arm upheld, like God. At the drop of his staff the whole circle would break the trance, lapsing back into quick march, reforming into column, and swinging on across the stadium again with that sure, majestic, almost stealthy swagger that comes to pipers. Then the long line of bugles, sweetly and movingly soft, sounding Retreat in their drawn-out falls of harmony to the hushed crowds.

But one topic remained to be touched upon before the month was out. This entailed explaining to the troops the purpose of the two identity discs with which all were issued, in the event of burial parties. The red one was to be cut from its cord around the neck and sent back for Records. The green one was to be buried with the man.

The bombers were now thundering across the Channel to their climax.

CHAPTER THREE

THE BLACK DOUGLAS AND OTHERS

THESE were Company Headquarters, or our old sweats. The Old Guard. Where stalked the figure of the Black Douglas.

He used to dwell within the Company stores, emerging only for important parades, and was in fact our Company storeman. Within his domain, entrenched behind a trestle table covered by an Army blanket and his tidy stacks of pants-woollen, oil bottles, boots, guncotton primers and other necessities of life, his power was absolute and rather frightening. Sergeants approached him with deference. Even the C.Q.M.S. spoke to him like one human being to another.

He was a dark, canny, rather fine looking man in his thirties, near enough to six feet, with a broad face, good features—especially nose and forehead—and a Lowlander's dark brown eyes that could show infinite and careful distrust. He had a dour, almost haughty reserve, but could look immensely expressive, and his confidants were strictly other old sweats—men like Mother Hickman, a frightening batman who nursed Duncan—who called him "Douggie" and to whom he would mutter.

A countryman from the west Borders, the skinning of minor animals, the lifting of fish from pools and the setting of snares and lines were second nature to him. One had no idea if he had a family: he seemed gauntly independent of the more intimate ties. His countryside was old in story, and always it seemed that an air of another age, of clamour, sword and hall, burnings, foray and Border rievers, attended him. He might have stepped from any page of Scott's minstrelsies, and in a more prosaic age at war he paid homage to none but the officer commanding "A" Company—to whom he gave his allegiance direct, like vassal before feudal overlord.

He disapproved of me for a long time. Until one day he was assisting me on training with various stores. We were left to walk home alone together at the end of the morning's work, and more from nervousness than anything else I heard myself quoting at him:

> The bloody heart blazed in the van,
> Announcing Douglas' dreaded clan.

I was immediately rewarded with a smile of unsuspected warmth. I had justified my existence. From that moment I was accepted by him and never looked back. . . .

However, the Black Douglas did not come to Europe with us at all. Shortly before D-Day he was posted to some special duty and his place in the stores was taken by a cheery chubby man from one of the platoons who had a wife and eight children in Ripon.

Jake was big and gruff and hailed from the Burns country. He had a face that seemed to be suffering perpetually from skin trouble, and his hair was skinned at the sides and stood up in a thick straight shock on top. His appearance was dreadfully fierce: a great shaggy fellow with no finesse whatever, and although not an old soldier you would take him for one.

Jake was downright, outspoken and apt to get angry. On duty he was originally the Company Commander's personal driver, and thus was exalted rather above our other drivers. Soon after I joined the Battalion I represented the O.C. "A" Company on a large Divisional night convoy exercise, where for hours we drove around through the night, with Jake at the wheel beside me, rugged and impassive. I struggled to stay awake and eventually fell asleep over my map-case. . . . "Gosh,

I could hardly keep my eyes open!" I remarked brightly next morning as we neared home again.

"Ay—I noticed that," was the crushing reply.

He was inflicted with particularly unattractive and troublesome teeth. Unwholesome yellow monsters they were, that eventually received their deserts. They vanished overnight and Jake went about with nothing to show except a pair of vicious upper canines standing sentinel, more wolf-like than ever. For many weeks he gnawed at his food and looked positively ferocious. Gradually one grew acclimatized to him. Then one day there he was, blushing to the roots of his hair in the Company Commander's truck, a coy smile revealing a magnificent new complement of dentures. Poor husky Jake. For a time he was so bashful he hardly dared open his mouth.

The advent of a jeep for the Company Commander, and with it a driver-batman, threatened a serious drop in prestige for him. Fortunately, more new toys were to be added to our transport in the shape of a couple of tracked carriers, and these were just the job for him. He was made first carrier driver, and we crossed to Normandy and went into action with the rugged Jake faithfully at his wheel, still with the constitutional authority of our Number One driver.

He was taken from the carrier with a piece of splinter in him when they were shelling us on a hill called 113, and that was the last we saw of him.

Then there was Johnstone 43. He was called Johnstone 43 to distinguish him from Johnstone 63, and Johnstone 75, and Johnstone 04, and all the other Johnstones. He came from somewhere around Gala, with a lilting, good-natured voice and a head that was very bald and pink. With an easy smile and the soft answer, he worked in the Company office as a second clerk and assisted the Black Douglas in the stores. But he, too, was a countryman, and the murmur of streams, the sighs of far woods and of breezes over the braes were in the soul of Johnstone 43, and in his voice. Especially streams. Streams with fish. The tributaries and waters of Tweed.

He also happened to be a crack rifle-shot, and was taken from us into the small team of battalion snipers run by the Intelligence Officer. Lord Wavell, it will be remembered, said that the ideal infantryman should be a combination of cat-burglar, gunman, poacher, with a seasoning of devilry in him, and Johnstone 43 was all these things in his gentle way.

Time and again he crept out ahead of the Battalion frontage in Normandy to ply his craft. There was another man with him: a leathery, burly, jolly man with remarkable pale blue eyes, who came also in the first place from "A" Company, called Bell. Corporal Bell. And very, very tough. The two worked as a pair—the snipers always worked in pairs. They were inseparable, and soon established a grim reputation for themselves. . . . Then Bell was killed. I saw him lying in a cart track near an orchard, covered by a gas cape with only his boots sticking out. And there was a shadow over the face of Johnstone 43 as he went his way, a look one had not seen there before; and he smiled less. And on across North-West Europe he went out, and laid up with his telescopic sights, and did deadly work. Bell must have been avenged a hundredfold. Long before the campaign was finished he had been awarded the Distinguished Conduct Medal, and his escapades were many. But all this he survived, to return to his braes and the streams of the Tweed, no longer of necessity Johnstone 43.

There was Mother Hickman. There was the long-suffering Rawden, the Company clerk; "A" Company literally turned his hair grey before he was finished with it.

And there was Andrew.

To all of us he was Andrew: Andrew and no more. Andrew was enough. One said, "Where's Andrew? . . ." One said, "Shout for Andrew. . . ." One said, "Tell Andrew. . . ." And one relied on Andrew.

I first met Andrew when taking the Company for a route march as a very new officer. At the end of the march, dismissing them in the usual way, I saw him grinning at me from the rear rank. Grinning at me while he sloped his rifle, turned to his right, slapped his butt and broke away. Furious, I called him back, keen to show that the new officer was not to be blatantly grinned at from the rear rank. I shouted at him.

"I could'na help it, sirr—it's my face, sirr," said Andrew. He was genuinely distressed. And later on I was to realize that he had been perfectly right. Extraordinarily enough, it was just Andrew's face.

He was a chirpy, stocky man who smoked a pipe, rather older than most of his comrades, and at one place where we were stationed he conducted a courtship with a vicar's housekeeper with a most successful outcome. By calling he was a Dumfriesshire farmworker, lined and weathered, with hands broad and strong that had a wonderful touch with animals. Whenever we had spent a night under the stars you would see Andrew at breakfast-time going to the nearest cow with his mess tin, to obtain fresh milk for his porridge. Perhaps he worked the beast's tail like a pump for the benefit of uninitiated onlookers. Often he would wander around whole unconcerned herds, appreciatively; in fact, Andrew's conversations with cattle were famous. And farm animals of all descriptions encountered during our travels, in any land, were a kind of challenge to him. If he found a stray horse, he had to ride it. He encouraged hens to lay eggs. Strange and unfriendly dogs trotted obediently at the sound of his voice.

Andrew—since I have mentioned his voice—never stopped talking. He never talked for an audience: he was quite happy talking to himself—or to animals. His flow of wit was endless, his tongue sharp and with a choice turn of phrase when he was feeling philosophical. That is, when browned off. At a moment's notice he could release an ever-ready flood of chatter, and on the line of march would swop life-histories with any bystander within the space of half a dozen incredible monosyllables snatched from the few seconds at his disposal as he passed by. Andrew never needed an answer—he could manage for two. In Europe the language difficulty did not affect him; in fact, Dutch sounded so similar to his broad native Scots as to be almost indistinguishable from it. But if you did not happen to be a Dutchman, Andrew's speech was not always easy to comprehend beyond the rapid reiteration of a familiar, overworked adjective without the free use of which he would have been severely handicapped.

Andrew, in short, was our perennial source of comic relief. A ludicrous portion of him had never grown up. Andrew was an especial kind of Peter Pan, shared by "A" Company and the beasts of the field. Every night of his life he slept in his tam o' shanter; a worn floppy object pulled at a special Andrew angle and endowed with almost supernatural qualities. It was his trademark; and his trade, that he could not help, was being the perfect example of a Jock. Through North-West Europe from start to finish he was present with "A" Company as Company runner; I can see him yet, in the paratrooper's wind-smock he had purloined from somewhere, when it was "Send Andrew. . . ." "Call Andrew. . . .", when all the humours and waywardness, and the worth of Jocks, seemed to materialize with Peter Pan Andrew.

CHAPTER FOUR

D-DAYS

THE sea front was deserted. I had returned late from Brighton by taxi, when out of the night came a low snarling of aero engines approaching from inland. Numbers of red navigation lights passed directly overhead, very low, moving smoothly out to sea southwestwards. The night was dark and the black shapes could hardly be made out against the sky, but their engines made an oppressive, heavy-laden sound, like Dakotas. The moving lights evenly distributed over the darkness and keeping formation with eerie consistency, the noise serving only to wrap them closer in the silence of that black sky. Across the invisible waters the dim red lights glided out and faded, and the engines died away, leaving night undisturbed again over the sleeping town. . . . And their snarl was "Overlord".

By daybreak the face of the world had altered. The airborne landings were already gone into history. The Second Front had opened.

We learnt about it early in the morning on the line of march, on the way to a rifle-range. And at the lunch break Gavin gave Duncan his head to tell the Company something about this new name, Normandy.

This was the sort of thing that Duncan, with his excitable, well-versed mind, was always good at, and he dearly loved imparting knowledge to the troops. In fact, Duncan had a personal interest in this invasion, for, like William the Conqueror, he too was descended from Rollo the Viking, First Duke of Normandy. Probably the opportunity to crusade to the soil of his forefathers tickled him quite a lot.

That evening the whole Mess gathered for the 9 o'clock News. Absurd to be sitting there listening to the B.B.C. on that tremendous Sixth of June, while the same Army of which we were part was engaging the enemy barely ninety miles from our windows. But the 15th Scottish were "Build Up".

There was a crush around the little table with someone's portable on it. . . . Upwards of thirty of us, mostly Scottish, with some Englishmen, three Canadians and a couple of Norwegians, plus a potent drop of Northern Irish in the person of Colonel Ben, who was apt to recall County Armagh, in fact, over his port. "J. D.", the senior Company Commander, coldly emaciated at the end of a slim cigarette holder. Seyton caught my eye from across the table: Seyton who commanded "C" Company with an easy humour and the light touch. Even Henry was satisfied. Henry had fought at Dunkirk with Colonel Ben, and Duncan, and Fred the Quartermaster; and Henry, a gentle man of almost comic tenacity, would have led "D" Company through hell itself to get back at the "bloody Boches".

A few days longer we remained in Worthing, while the battle mounted beyond that horizon. Each fresh day was a D-Day for us. We were ready. There was nothing to detain us except the tides and the timetables. And on the fourth evening the Second-in-Command was seen driving out of the town in his jeep with everything waterproofed to the eyebrows. Another peacetime soldier, he was a type who looked as though he ought never to be away from old tweeds and fishing-tackle. But Giles was not going fishing this time. He was going to stake out our ground in the concentration area on the other side, with the Divisional advance-parties.

The next morning we ceased to be a battalion.

We passed into the arms of Movement Control. In the eyes of Movement Control there were no such things as brigades, battalions, regiments or companies. Movement Control viewed everything in terms of boatloads. To them the invasion armies were so many bodies. Bodies that had to be fed, rested, medically administered to if they fell ill—and sorted into boatloads. Then sent to the nearest port of embarkation—with a "Mae West" per body in case the boat was sunk, and three bags-vomit for seasickness—and embarked as fast as the weather and shipping turnover would allow. On the other side their counterpart, Beach Control, then contrived the reverse process, and all the bodies were miraculously "married up" again into brigades, battalions, regiments and companies: ready for battle.

The advance parties and the guns and vehicles vanished towards London for embarkation at Tilbury. The infantry, carrying their worldly possessions on their backs, were collected into various marshalling camps in the Sussex hinterland.

Installed in a camp near Lewes, we were faced with more D-Days. Altogether three of them. Once we had a false alarm and paraded for departure, only to be stood down again. There was nothing to do but lie in the sun when it shone or in our tents when it rained, and eat enormous meals served by the permanent staff.

The camp was situated in the grounds of a large house. Within the house, inevitably, sat Movement Control, in communication with Newhaven harbour, plotting over their timetables. "A" Company had not been split up, but together with most of "C" Company had become Boat Serial Number 24067. All day the loudspeakers through the camp broadcast summonses and instructions to boat commanders, and whenever 24067 cropped up Gavin stumped off to the big house to present himself before Movement Control. Gavin, being senior rank on our prospective boat, was the boat commander, or O.C. Troops. However, this only applied to internal discipline among the troops. The man responsible for taking us to the brink of a Normandy beach, selected in the last resort by himself, was the Naval officer in command of the ship. While afloat his judgment was supreme, even, it appeared, if he had a boatload of Generals. Gavin, with all his instincts as a regular soldier rising to the nice juxtaposition of authority was a great stickler for this.

"The Captain can say to me I cannot land you *there*, I shall have to land you *there*," he explained in a talk to the Company. "But I, if necessary, could reply that *there* the situation ashore is such that I cannot undertake to disembark my troops."

It looked as if the Naval Captain had not the power actually to make us get off his ship, once on, and that if he beached us at some point navigable but where we should only rush off into the jaws of unreasonable death, Gavin could cause us all to return to England again in angry deadlock. Luckily such an eventuality was not to arise.

One evening Danny and I went for a walk through the woods around the camp, and Danny talked about Hawick; and the next afternoon, the eighth day after D-Day, the loudspeakers again told Serial Number 24067 to stand by for embarkation. Again we paraded and rehearsed putting on the Mae Wests; the girding on of these lifebelts the one stark shaft of down-to-earth reality in the great dreamlike drama of those tingling early June days. But this time bags-vomit were issued all round, and were promptly used for wrapping up the rations for the voyage. And as a parting gift from Blighty, in each man's possession was a tin of foot powder.

We boarded waiting lorries and were convoyed straight to Newhaven. Through villages of waving people and the country town of Lewes, where quite a crowd was watching the convoys, we came to the harbour. It was crammed with little ships.

All were Landing Craft Infantry, with a capacity of some two hundred men, and a ramp on either side of the bows for disembarkation. All had made the crossing on D-Day, and on their small fo'c'sles was painted the sign of the Tyne and Tees Division, of North Africa fame, whose troops they had carried over. Our own boat had had both her ramps blown off by underwater mines, but otherwise showed no evidence of damage. Built in the U.S.A. in 1942, this slender little ship had sailed the world. She had carried G.I.s across the Pacific, and taken part in the Sicily landings. Her crew were now R.N.V.R.

On board there was a tremendous, scarcely suppressed air of excitement, a running buffet in the ship's galley, ample and ingenious washing facilities, and enormous quantities of tinned food. Much of it had been left over by the assault troops. There were tins of chocolate, tins of self-heating cocoa—tins of every conceivable nourishment. The tiny upper deck was out of bounds to troops, but as a courtesy our officers were allowed on to it. Duncan, with tongue firmly in cheek, consequently spread it that we were allowed "upstairs"—and that the officers' cabin was "downstairs at the back end".

"Did you hear that chap?" they breathed at one another on the bridge.

And late in the evening we put out to sea.

As we glided through the still water of Newhaven harbour, two pipers appeared right forward in the bows of each ship. We approached the breakwater and passed it to the sound of the bagpipes. Once more it was the slow plaintive lilt of the "Skye Boat Song", whose only accompaniment was the slight throb of the engines, a bell from the bridge, and the wash lapping back to the quaysides. The Channel breezes met us and the pipes sounded over the water, clear and lonely, then ceased. Westwards the last sheen of daylight was going out of the sky, and there was one star. The high white cliffs receded away into the gloom. On the upper deck a young Naval signaller was on watch beside me. One could only distinguish the silhouette of his cap and dufflecoat, and the pale glimmer of his face, in the one starlight. It was already night. A light from a dark bulk of cliff winked morse across the water and was answered from the bridge. It was 10.50pm, on the 14th of June. The little ships crept away into the Channel. . . .

We were in the keeping of the Navy. With deft efficiency they carried out their job.

The Captain was a fresh-faced lieutenant-commander, R.N.V.R., and had two or three officers at his side on the bridge. The course was roughly thirteen miles out to sea, then parallel with the coast until we were off Portsmouth, then straight over to Normandy. The voyage was a very fair picnic.

By morning, in mid-Channel, our convoy seemed to have grown. From horizon to horizon other convoys were plying towards the Normandy coast, or returning for more. Unobtrusively to either side of us dipped and ploughed a grey, terse escort of destroyers. Ships were in all directions, dotted away to distant smudges of smoke until somewhere in the seventies one lost count. Of hostile interference there was no trace, but the vigilance of the Navy never relaxed. The ship's officers stayed glued to the bridge.

"What's that on the port side?" asked Alastair, getting knowledgeable, pointing over the right-hand rail. "Starboard, please!" he was told.

At one moment something floated past that closely resembled a submarine periscope. We pointed it out to the Captain with a certain diffidence, more as a matter of interest. Without a word he sprang to his binoculars and gave it a hard scrutiny. It was a piece of wreckage.

A hazy grey outline arose ahead. The soldiers clambered on deck for their first look at France.

"How was it on the Sixth?" one asked a sparse, trim Petty Officer.

"Sick all over the place," he said. "Hardly had the strength to crawl through the waves to the beach, getting knocked down and shot at," he said. "Poor devils."

We drew closer to the shore, in past the anchored cruisers and under the guns of H.M.S. *Ramillies*, to a short distance off the sands. It was low tide. Because of the blown ramps some of us would have to get wet, but some amphibious

DUKWs were coming out from the beach. The lieutenant-commander relaxed for the first time since Newhaven. He called out to Gavin by rank and name over his loudspeaker from the bridge

"Good Luck!" he called, with a depth of sincerity in odd contrast to his cool, dispassionate handling of the voyage, and a long stare across the water to Gavin—now bobbing about in his DUKW some way away. And from the dwindling figure of Gavin an arm was raised in laconic acknowledgment.

Most of 7 Platoon piled into another DUKW that quickly deposited us high and dry enough on a damp stretch of sand. We jumped out and our boots were upon Normandy soil. Others less fortunate had to wade ashore. We were a few miles east of the Mulberry harbour at Arromanches.

The beaches were a scene of astonishingly calm activity. It was early afternoon; the sun was out, and hot. Beach Group personnel and parties of Sappers were everywhere moving about unconcernedly in their shirt-sleeves or stripped to the waist. Other landing craft were disembarking more infantry, tank-landing ships were yielding their cargoes of vehicles and heavy equipment down great ramps. Metal roadstrips had been laid up to the hinterland. DUKWs and jeeps buzzed to and fro among churning lorries and heavy breakdown recovery vehicles. Barrage balloons were aloft along the whole shore. And of a battle there was no sign. Not a gunshot, not a Messerschmitt. Nobody seemed concerned. At first sight it looked a methodical unflustered chaos that might have been some fantastic novelty at Blackpool. Seawards it was a little different. Forlorn groups of masts and funnels, listing hulls with decks awash, and the occasional hulks of "drowned" or blown up vehicles and other bits and pieces among the anti-tank stakes, told their story.

We were filed into a kind of sheep-pen. Near by, surprisingly undamaged, was a small farm a bare hundred yards from the shore. A Frenchman in a blue smock moved about, tenaciously attending to his pigs. He turned a dour, non-committal back on us. They were waiting to see how long we would stay, these dark peasants of Normandy. . . . Behind the farm a wide field was surrounded by a single strand of barbed wire on posts. A white board was fixed to one of the posts, on which a skull and crossbones were painted black. Underneath, the words

Achtung! Minen!

In the sheep-pen Gavin was given the map route we were to follow. As "A" Company again we set out for the Battalion's concentration area, some five miles march inland. . . . So we turned into France, skirting the minefield up a track the way the assault had gone nine days before. A certain amount of litter, old bags-vomit, and battered ration-packs lay about, and at the side of the track was a soiled, discarded Mae West. There was blood on it.

CHAPTER FIVE

THE PROUD

WE marched inland through the hot dusty afternoon. The calm that had reigned over the beaches continued until we entered Creully, where there was an abrupt interruption. There was little damage here and the inhabitants had remained, and welcomed us very differently from the few stray countryfolk we had passed. The blameless little place had become Army Group tactical headquarters, but besides this distinction was fairly galvanized by commotion. Columns of marching infantry were trudging through the main street, while a long convoy of "flail" tanks, their massive steel chains hanging dormant from the great axles protruding before their hulls, lurched and clattered down the centre of the roadway, swirling up dust. All was hearteningly going inland. The population thronged their doorways or ran excitedly alongside us with greetings and handshakes.

Then we were into the countryside again. At a halt a youth in a beret with a small boy came and sat down among us. The first Frenchman to speak to. Could one find the good beer and cider in Normandy? He shrugged. "Les Boches tout bu!" chimed in the small boy.

Someone gave the elder one a cigarette. "Where are the Boches, alors?"

Another shrug, and a vague wave of the hand:

"En Allemagne."

So far as he was concerned.

Beyond a small village called St Gabriel, Giles, the Second-in-Command, emerged into view. We were deflected into a large placid field surrounded by high, almost impenetrable hedgerows. Here the Battalion would concentrate, and as the Companies arrived at intervals from the beaches they were set to bivouac under the cover of the great hedges. In the middle of the field cows grazed, and would moon across to drink at a trough close to where "A" Company found themselves. From time to time a herdsman materialized to tend to them, but neither he nor some young farmworkers at the crops the other side of our hedge attempted to fraternize. We settled down for a strange kind of holiday that was to last over a week, in which Track Discipline became one of the main features of life. We were completely hedgebound, and any comings and goings across the centre of the field or anywhere away from a hedge were rigorously forbidden, against tell-tale pathways through the long grass warning enemy aircraft of our presence. We ate, slept, paraded and generally had our being in the lee of those dense hedgerows. And waited to be called into battle.

As for the war, one probably knew rather less about it than the people back home. Scarcely a breath even of the gales that now whipped the Channel penetrated into this sequestered field, and newspapers, several days old from England, were devoured to find out what was happening. Around us, below our perplexingly peaceful horizon, the hidden armies fought amid a land dissected by its countless orchards, hedges and paddocks. But only occasional, graphic but disconnected bits of news filtered back to us.

The first intimations of battle sounded from the rear gun-positions of the Polar Bear Division, who were holding the immediate part of the line ahead of us. At various inconsequential hours, often in the stillness of evening, invariably in the cold dawn, a battery thumped into life, loosed off a few salvoes, and subsided again, perhaps 800 to 1000 yards away among the fields beyond our field, called by some crisis in which lives were at stake. We could only hear them fire. The crash of the shells exploding was much too far away. But as we lay securely in our blankets of an early morning,

Germans, somewhere, were likely dying. The thumps, dispassionate acts of mechanical precision employed in killing, manipulated by hands as human as your own, that the next minute would be lifting mugs of tea and lighting cigarettes. At first it was quite unbelievable, with something grotesquely animate to the mind's eye about the hidden gun-barrels as they reared alert, ready to prick up, and pounce, and kill. One afternoon a set attack evidently went in, and the thumps kept up a more sustained activity.

At night there was a far more picturesque and exhilarating reminder of the battle. In the small hours the Luftwaffe made its appearance, to bomb the beaches and drop mines among the shipping. The field was on rising ground and gave a wonderful view of the sky. With incredible speed the red tracers of the "flak" leaped into the night, like strings of bubbles up a champagne glass, from innumerable guns, weaving fantastic patterns in the sky. In and out, the mosquito-drone of an aircraft, and periodically the great, far "crump" and sudden glare, where a stick had landed. Then an Ack-Ack battery in the next field opened up and hammered the night, shaking the earth we lay on, then more and more, following the planes, until the whole dark countryside was awake and barking. . . . Each night sleep was shattered with a jump and we witnessed this display.

A limited programme of airings was soon instituted to keep everyone on his toes, and on various occasions we set foot outside the field. A daily route march and some liberty trips into Bayeux speedily gave a truer view of the situation inland of the immediate beach areas. The full implication of the Normandy bridgehead now broke over us. For this brief time we were the onlookers.

"We shall never see this again," we said. Enormous quantities of men and material had already been put ashore. Colossal masses of equipment had been established behind the battle line. The entire countryside seemed packed to capacity with the build-up of operations. No usable acre was left untouched by men and engines. A truck travelling the highway from Creully to Bayeux passed no field bare of gun sites. The communications sped down every road, and the signal cables, and the "Verges Cleared" boards. At every turn appeared the hierarchy of formation signs in all their profusion of heraldry, culminating in the Crusader's Cross and crossed swords of the Army Group shield. Over all, a tremendous sense of mission. There was a finality; and the soldier who marched those sullen, dust-littered routes that led to "the line" in Normandy—Hat Route, Star Route, Sun Route, they were legion—felt his place in history as he trod into battle beside his God. And although actual immersion in the fighting narrowed the perspective, and the shock of immediate realities and the dull burden of staying alive oppressed and riveted the mind, this feeling—"we're on a mighty mission" as the song borrowed from the Pacific went—was never lost.

As for our own Division, hardly an individual except for the Commanders and a sprinkling of senior ranks had seen action before. Consequently we savoured this enforced prelude to the full. *Esprit de corps* at the highest pitch. The troops in amazing spirits. For here was the Second Front. We were upon the rostrum of the world. At last, after the months and years of waiting whilst others went out, we too were out, to take part of deeds. Now all was justified. This was our place, this close-packed bridgehead, beside those already here. With the British Western Expeditionary Force. The words persisted: "Gentlemen in England. . . ." The lines came back:

> And gentlemen in England now a-bed
> Shall think themselves accursed they were not here,
> And hold their manhoods cheap whiles any speaks
> That fought with us. . . .

These were wonderful moments.

Then the visits to Bayeux. The town once fallen to Rollo the Viking was in its first flush of liberation. In the doorway of a little shop one is assailed by the inevitable request for a cigarette. One turns, and sees a frail old lady in long black garments seated in the shadows. An entrance just inside the shop leads to the living-quarters, and from there she surveys the busy scene in the street outside.

"You have no cigarettes?" you ask her curiously.

Apparently not. For your own part you want postcards. There are no postcards either.

"Les Boches tout pris," the ancient voice croaks in complaint.

It was the cry everywhere.

But the enemy had hardly left starvation in their wake. Bayeux fairly flowed with the dairy produce of a rich countryside. We bought voraciously. There was everything, including a vegetable the Jocks called "artic-choos"—and a prolific yield of ripe Camembert cheeses, *Fabriqué en Normandie*. After wartime rationing at home, these were like works of art. But, puzzlingly, the troops disliked Camembert. After my first trip into Bayeux I made the mistake of distributing a number of these cheeses around 7 Platoon, where, alas, they were soon diagnosed as not being in the normal run of perishables that go with Army biscuits and by an obscure process of conservatism rejected. Camembert was obviously officers' food.

Bayeux was undamaged, and among the carefree motley in the quaint old streets the pulse of life beat quick. Apart, in the calm of a by-water, stood the cathedral. Here, encased under the cool serenity of stone, was a replica of the Tapestry. The original having been "pris".

The first alert for action came a day or two after we landed, and the Battalion "Order" group ominously disappeared on a reconnaissance. Late in the evening they returned, and Gavin sent for the platoon commanders and their sergeants. We assembled in his bivouac, a rigged-up vehicle tarpaulin that he shared with Duncan. Maps were taken out. We could scarcely see one another for the dusk, and we all watched the little circle of torchlight on Gavin's map-board. Gavin sat on a box with the map-board across his knees and began to propound. I wanted to shiver. Gavin was blunt and grave.

The prospect sounded unpleasant. We were moving off the next day to attack across the low-lying ground beyond the Orne river, on the extreme left flank of the bridgehead. The ground had been taken by the Airborne on D-Day, but lost again. We would be attacking through the Highland Division, who had been having a sticky time of it. The whole area was under enemy observation. There was no time for platoon commanders to see the ground beforehand and we must show our men their objectives as best we could from the forming-up places, which would probably be under fire. The object of the operation was the envelopment of Caen from the north and east. We pored over the maps with our torches. I still wanted to shiver, but the others looked all right. We were all very normal.

The next day the operation was cancelled.

In some relief we resumed existence in our field. Reading the old papers from home. Living for the call "Mail up!" The solace of writing letters. The delicate task of censoring the troops' letters, accepted on both sides with a tacit honour. And the few minor training activities. The days began to pass. Days with expeditions to neighbouring farms on endless barter for vegetables, milk and cream. Seventy bars of chocolate levied from the platoon on one occasion to be traded for dozens of eggs. A group of Jocks frying onions in butter. A child snatched indoors as one approached a farmyard, and the ramparts of suspicion that had to be scaled to reach these people. A splendid château revealed down a lane that made the war seem out of place. The long column of "A" Company wending its way on pilgrimage to a Mobile Bath Unit, where portable boilers tethered to some stream bellowed breath into a marquee through an Emmett-like system of pipes that resulted in hot showers. And always straining for news of the battle, and listening to the thumps ahead—and accosting two R.E.M.E. sergeants in a jeep with the Polar Bear sign on their shoulders:

"What's it like in front?"

"Pretty sticky."

We were always in the dark.

Then Gavin in tremendous form one evening, hailing me into his bivouac for a giant whisky. Duncan rather disapproving, and irritating. Duncan delegating one Corporal Macbeth in my platoon as "A" Company official interpreter in French. And Macbeth, a man from Banff, whose paybook gave his former trade as Civil Servant, going about officially interpreting over my head. None of us knew much French, but I knew mine to be the equal of Macbeth's—indeed superior to Macbeth's. So did Duncan. I was touchy about my French. Duncan knew that too.

The next alert was the real thing. A set-piece showdown with ample preparation.

Nowhere was the difference between Gavin and Duncan more typical than over the procedure known as "Painting the Picture". Duncan painted a Big Picture, with swift large flourishes in keeping with the grandiloquent conception of the man. He loved doing it, and could certainly give an extraordinarily well-presented and interesting background to the more detailed arrangements made for 7, 8 and 9 Platoons of "A" Company.

Gavin, laconic and matter-of-fact considered that 7, 8 and 9 Platoons should damned well know enough to enable them to do what they were told to do, and that regaling them with overmuch Big Picture was probably a waste of time.

There is no doubt that Duncan's practice was infinitely more appreciated. But Gavin was obstinate. At length Platoon commanders and their sergeants presented themselves in a plaintively deferential body before his bivouac:

"But what's actually happening, sir?"

"Sar'major, what are these subalterns and sergeants running around for?" the voice of Gavin was heard edgily inquiring after blandly dismissing us with some non-committal assurance. He had already arranged to assemble the whole Company.

The Company were gathered.

This time it was to be a drive on the west side of Caen, and would be the largest operation yet mounted in Normandy, extending to a frontage of three corps that was finally to include Caen itself, with 15th Scottish Division leading to punch the hole for an armoured break-out. For this the Division were to have a Churchill tank brigade and special detachments of other heavy assault vehicles—or "Funnies"—in support, and one of the greatest artillery barrages since Alamein. The enemy on our front were the 12th SS Panzer Division: the Hitler Youth. "Their chief desire," says Gavin, pointer in hand by a map on a blackboard, "is to die for their Fuhrer—and they will shortly be given every opportunity to do so." Good man, Gavin! The Company like that. There is a laugh. "The air support," finishes Gavin, in his down-to-earth style, "is to be the whole of the Tactical Air Force." Yes. Gavin could put over the stuff to give the troops. . . . This time there were no misgivings.

We were to attack through 3rd Canadian Division from forward assembly areas around the village of Bretteville l'Orgueilleuse. This lay some nine miles inland from the beaches and five out of Caen, up the straight ruler-line of the Caen-Bayeux main highway. The Canadians had reached it on D plus 1, and there the battle-line had held. The various Company reconnaissance parties from the Lowland Brigade arrived at discreet intervals during the next day or so, and here we found true devastation. The civilians had long since fled, and Bretteville, straddling the main road, was left to rot. Houses and cottages stood crazily pitted, or gaping under shattered roofs with slate, plaster and rubble spilled around. Not a building had been overlooked.

We left the jeep behind and progressed on foot, well spread out, up a straight little road in the direction of the enemy: the "A" Company party consisting of Gavin and his officers, all armed with rifles, maps and binoculars. On the right was a huge sixty-ton German Panther tank, miraculously heaved on to its back by some local cataclysm, its broken tracks and bogies mutely useless against the sky. Further to the right an open field was strewn with the charred hulls of brewed-up British Shermans. We crossed a main railway line, deserted except for a few pieces of splintered rolling-stock, and passed a lone calvary with a solitary grave near by. After a few hundred yards up a gentle gradient we came to a tiny subsidiary village named Norrey. It was little more than a farm hamlet. A shrapnel-splattered board proclaimed the church for the benefit of tourists: "Norrey. Merveille du XII Siècle"—a miniature gem with a once beautiful interior of white stone. Now tower, roof—all caved in, and the tiny nave a chaotic heap of masonry, the altar buried. The hamlet a forward Canadian outpost.

There was a thick, uneasy quiet. Now and then a figure slunk between the buildings on an errand for water cans or on its way to a command post. One of them was unaptly ensconced over a latrine pit. There was no talk. It was mid-afternoon and the sun beat down, and stubble was on faces and that watchful look when a man knows if he shows his head he gets a piece of lead through it. We met Hugh, the I.O., who was already up there, and who introduced us to the Canadian Company Commander in his command post.

"As long as you fellers don't bunch, and go quiet," they told us. "We get mortared if we show any movement, but it's all right if you keep to the houses. . . ."

We clambered through a farmyard into the shambles of a house, and keeping well back from the yawning windows on the upper floor, with our camouflage veils pulled over our faces, looked beyond. There before us were the rolling cornlands, with their great hedgerows, trees and clumps of wood, and the concealed villages of that awful country that was to become known as the Scottish Corridor. We knitted ourselves to our maps, then gazed beyond the window again, keeping right back against the opposite wall. . . . The hidden stream called the Muc. . . . St Manvieu. . . . La Gaule. . . . Cheux. . . . Names on the map. Names in all their foreboding, screened from us, brooding there among the pregnant cornfields. And rising out of distant trees, like fate, we could just see the top of St Manvieu church tower. . . .

"Look just in front of that wood," said Hugh—"you can see the head of a sentry." Far in front was a tiny dot on the ground.

"You can make him out through the binoculars," said Hugh.

I raised my binoculars. Very small, but quite clear, was a distant Wehrmacht helmet level with the top of a slit-trench. It moved slightly. The first German of the war that I had set eyes on. There, whoever he was, my enemy.

Then we went out into an adjoining orchard. Extending further again from this was the start line for our attack. There was a hedge around the orchard, and a Canadian platoon had positions here. Never had we seen slit-trenches dug so deep. Fire steps had been built in order to see out of them, while burrowed into the soil off the trench floors were recesses in which the men not on stand-to were sleeping.

"Don't go up to the hedge," we were warned. They added that enough unprintable came down on them in the ordinary course of events.

"What causes most of the casualties?" one asked a sergeant. "Nearly all mortars."

A man had been killed shortly before we arrived.

They were tough, these Canadians. There was a good deal of night-patrol activity on both sides, and the Canadians went out in gym shoes for increased stealth. The SS had also been shooting their wounded, which angered them bitterly, and they retaliated.

They were helpful and only worried about our drawing fire on to them, and we left them to it again. We had done our best for their sakes, but something must have been seen, for they got another dose soon afterwards.

The next day platoon parties went up, again at well-staggered times and with further admonitions for stealth. We showed our sergeants and section leaders the same objectives. The Canadians were commendably patient, realizing the big attack was coming.

"Look just in front of that wood," I directed MacEwan and Co. of 7 Platoon—"you can see the head of a sentry. . . ." MacEwan, Corporal Nim, a big lance-sergeant called Duke, and Macbeth: they looked.

Then, following the same route as the Company party had gone the day before, we returned towards Bretteville, down a track parallel to the little road by which we had entered Norrey, and which was actually our outward axis for the attack.

Recrossing the railway line, I pointed to a large cornfield behind us, to pass on another piece of information from the day before: "There's a spandau post over there," I remarked, and was astonished to find myself alone. The four N.C.O.s were already in the ditch, having assumed the hostile machine-gun was covering us and jumped for it with the speed of light. After this misunderstanding we continued back to the jeep.

By the upturned Panther of the day before a burly Canadian Sapper sergeant was making a dump of dismantled German tellermines.

"Have you seen any corpses yet, boys?" he was most eager to know.

We had not.

"I'll show you some!" he said. "Over in the field there. Three Jerries. Lovely! Been there a week. Dead black and stomachs out to here"—and he drew a bloated gesture with his arms.

We said we would see plenty later on, thanks, and went

49

home. I took a tellermine with me, thinking it might be of use to "A" Company in brushing up their mine recognition, and proudly laid it before Gavin's bivouac. Whereupon Gavin bade the sergeant-major chuck the thing away.

From the moment we landed, the Brigadier, whose famous sprint will be remembered, had spent his time going forward to the battle to see other brigades and glean what he could for us. Now he visited us in our field and gathered every officer and N.C.O. to a corner around him. Officers and N.C.O.s, he said among other things, would not wear their badges of rank into battle. Too many leaders had been lost through advertising their rank to enemy snipers. We would not go into this battle conspicuous in any way from the private soldiers. "Now, I don't want to lose any of my officers or N.C.O.s because of carelessness."

He was sitting on a ration box in his balmoral and shirtsleeves. We were sprawled on the grass. He was being almost fatherly. His medals were three from World War I and a D.S.O. from France, 1940. And one liked the way "carelessness" had come out. Of course there would be casualties—but well, one must just not be careless. Let us think of it like that. The "Brig" suddenly seemed very safe. And we stood up and saluted him as he left for his next battalion.

The last day in the field pressed heavily. The men sat about writing their letters while the sun set. I went for a stroll with Bruce the carrier officer, who told shaggy dog stories. There was also comfort in dipping into the poems of A. E. Housman and a Kipling anthology, the two books in my kit.

The next day the sun set on the Battalion swinging out of the field for the last time, for battle.

The columns tramped through a dusty June evening to its dusk, and the sun went. In darkness we came to the assembly area by a village named Secqueville, where there was a hot drink and an issue of soup. It was also a gun area, and we lay down to rest in our weapon slits under the very gun muzzles. They fired deafeningly at intervals throughout the night, so there was little sleep. At one o'clock it began to rain, thinly. Soon we fell in, and the march continued to the forward assembly area at Bretteville l'Orgueilleuse. Bretteville the Proud. Which epithet, sadly, lighted upon the men who marched that night.

CHAPTER SIX

INTO BATTLE

EVERY detail of the day was printed indelibly on the memory. Our first action, 26th June 1944. . . .

Arriving from Secqueville into the forward assembly area. 3am in the drizzling rain. Pitch dark, with the minute-hand slipping leadenly to the dawn. Digging shallow pits as a precaution against enemy counter-shelling, and huddled with my batman, head to toe, with our anti-gas capes spread over us for some warmth. Then more fitful sleep, until at 5.30 the sentries stole around the silent positions with muttered words, shaking the inert figures in the ground back to consciousness.

We woke dully, shivering. Still dark, and the drizzle still falling. With two hours to the barrage.

The blowing of the petrol cooker sounded from the barn, where the cooks were preparing breakfast. Then a subdued jangle of mess tins, the occasional glow of a cigarette end, and a straggling queue of men with slung rifles: shadowy blurs forming for porridge, "compo" sausages, biscuits and tinned margarine, and a mug of steaming tea, in the first glimmer of dawn.

Inside the barn on some sacks sat the Company officers. We ate and said little. Gavin, weather-beaten, with the steady grey eyes. Duncan, whose big moustache was suddenly obvious again, although one had seen it a thousand times. They exchanged trivialities without a word about the battle. Danny, Alastair and myself swopping desultory comments of a more relevant kind—

"Hour and a half to the barrage. . . ."

"Weather's bad for flying. . . ."

"Any more 'chah'? . . ."

The sergeant-major, stocky and stubbly chinned, uttering brisk and inconsequent remarks about the coming attack, with no one particularly listening to him. His dark eyes restless. Switching from one to the other of us, watching us. A wife and two kids back in Edinburgh.

One performed Nature's duty in an adjacent cabbage patch. It struck me as oddly unnecessary. Gavin came across to do likewise.

"Perhaps they won't start shelling until the barrage opens?" I asked him. For the enemy were quiet. He raised his eyebrows. How the hell could he say?

It was becoming quite light. The drizzle had stopped, but there was a mist. We cursed the mist. No help to the Tactical Air Force.

Green camouflage cream was shared out in grubby palms and smeared over our faces—we never bothered to use it again. Weapons were carefully cleaned and oiled. Magazines loaded. Bayonets fixed. Midday rations—slabs of bully beef and cheese with more biscuits—packed into haversacks. The boiled sweets and chocolate stowed into a handy pocket. Cigarette tins into another. . . . The men quietly chatting and smoking in little groups, in their platoons. Everyone admirably controlled, but an air of tension about them. None quite knew what battle would be like. And we waited for H Hour.

The minute hand touched 7.30. . . . On the second, nine hundred guns of all calibres, topped by the fifteen-inch broadsides from the distant battleships lying off the beaches, vomited their inferno. Concealed guns opened from fields, hedges and farms in every direction around us, almost as if arranged in tiers. During short pauses between salvoes more guns could be heard, and right away, further guns, filling and reverberating the very atmosphere with a sustained, muffled hammering. It was like rolls of thunder, only it never slackened. Then the guns near by battered out again with loud, vicious, strangely mournful repercussions. The thunder angry, violent and death-dealing. Hurling itself over strong-points, enemy gun areas, forming-up places, tank laagers, and above all concentrated into the creeping mass of shells that raked ahead of our own infantrymen, as thousands of gunners bent to their task. Little rashes of goose-flesh ran over the skin. One was hot and cold, and very moved. All this "stuff" in support of us! Every single gun at maximum effort to kill; to help us.

Now the Company were forming up to move off: the Battalion initially to be in support, as a second and "mopping up" wave on the heels of the "Royals" and the "Fusiliers". We shouted to hear ourselves speak. We were in a fantastic world of unbelief. We felt nervously energetic. Officers and sergeants must preserve calm exteriors, appear pointedly casual; but the effort of shouting orders above the din spoilt the effect. The Jocks felt the moment. Some joked—goodness knows what about, but it didn't matter. Some stood silent, smiling apart as they just listened to the enormous effort of the guns. All were joined by a most poignant undercurrent of emotion that obliterated rank. All were smoking. It was steadying to smoke. I felt I should be saying heroic words of encouragement to 7 Platoon, but words were superfluous.

"Now's your chance to get your own back for all the time you've been shoved around in the army!" I got out. They grinned, likely not hearing properly. Alastair was saying something to 9 Platoon.

Gavin came over, stolidly puffing at his pipe. Over there was Duncan with Company Headquarters, going like a furnace.

"All right," from Gavin, briefly.

"Right, sir."

We moved off.

Still no enemy counter-battery fire—then at that moment a new noise. Yes—there they were, shelling the forming-up place and start line, and the Canadians again. The noise was lost once more in the thunder over our heads.

So down a small winding road, with the absurd feeling that it was just another exercise. Only guns were not thundering before. Then a cold sensation in the pit of the stomach. The "enemy" were the 12th SS. We had been told so. And as if in confirmation we passed the Battalion medical sergeant at the wayside, his red-cross armband exceedingly obvious. Exchanging repartee with the marching men. And a little further on, Colonel Ben. Ben in steel helmet, belt and revolver holster over a mackintosh, and carrying a walking-stick. Ben who had known Dunkirk, watching his Battalion march into action. He stepped with Gavin for a while at the head of the Company, then stood aside to watch us go by. His face stern, but with a word and a smile of recognition here and there for a man who passed.

We came to shattered Bretteville, and crossing the Caen-Bayeux main road followed the axis of attack down the lane parallel to the road to Norrey. Again past the charred and scattered hulls of the Shermans, strewn about over the field that was now revealed as a minefield with warning boards spaced around it. Along the verges were some blown-up bren carriers. All these sorry wrecks, it was noted, being "ours". To the left front were the ruins of Norrey village once more. On the right a farm which looked as though a vast hammer had struck it a sharp blow. We crossed the railway and deployed into a large ploughed field. It was the forming-up place.

Still the guns thundered. Ahead an explosive, chaotic din could vaguely be heard where the receiving end of the barrage churned its way forward in hundred-yard lifts. Close behind it would be the two leading battalions. The first wave of the assault. As close as they could to the shells, through the mist. And again we cursed the mist. "The whole of the Tactical Air Force," and not a plane in the sky.

In the forming-up place there was a short wait. "A" and "B" Companies, leading the Battalion with "C" and "D" in support, shook out into formation for the advance, then got down with entrenching tools to scrape protection pits.

The field rose gently to a low skyline, that was the start line running on the left into the orchard where we had made our reconnaissance. Neatly above Norrey a number of swirling black puffs of smoke appeared, to the sound of cruel, heavy detonations.

Crump! . . . Crump! . . . Crump!—Crump!—Crump! . . .

German shrapnel air-bursts.

"Get down—stop walking about!"

I was being yelled at by Gavin, having been strolling around the platoon while they scraped their pits, determined to remain casual.

We lay for about ten minutes, watching the air-bursts over some tall trees in the orchard. More appeared over Norrey. Then stray figures in battle-dress materialized out of the mist, coming back from the battle. Each with levelled bayonet prodding two or three helmetless and sullen, bewildered-looking youths in grimy camouflage smocks and trousers. They held their hands in a resigned, tired way above their blond heads.

Germans!

A miracle anything could have lived through the stunning they had taken, and a testimony to the efficacy of the slit-trench.

We stared after them: trying to comprehend the actuality of our enemies. A Regimental Provost corporal, taking charge of one, flicked him contemptuously across the shoulders with his driving-gauntlets, rearwards. And morale soared. Prisoners already! Things must be going well. The sight did a world of good to the younger ones among us, upon whom the strain of composure had been beginning to tell.

Then Colonel Ben's word came over the wireless. Gavin relayed us the signal. . . . "The Battalion will Advance. . . ."

We arose and moved up the field in extended line of sections. There was a lull in the air-bursts. We came level with the orchard. The wide fields of ripening corn rolled away before us, the mist already lifting to an overcast sky of low cloud. Then past the Canadian outposts and stray incoming parties of Canadians who had been out, gate-crashing the battle, helping to bring home the wounded.

"Rifles at the hip—safety catches off!" you shouted.

Two motionless figures were sprawled near by. A glimpse of twisted legs in SS canvas, a crooked arm, a swollen belly—and you looked away again, ahead. We were past the start line, and moving forward through the corn.

CHAPTER SEVEN

ENCOUNTER

THE barrage ceased, leaving an oppressive stillness. The guns reverting to regimental control, on call to the infantry as required. Our boots now treading towards that wriggling black line in the newspaper diagrams and the war maps of Allied councils.

I travelled with my runner with the right leading section. We trampled on watchfully through the high thick corn. Sergeant Duke's section some hundred yards to our left. Macbeth's men following behind, and behind them Tam MacEwan and the rest of Platoon Headquarters. Further to the left, 8 Platoon. Behind again, Gavin, with his wireless, signallers and runner. Then 9 Platoon, and Duncan, and rear Company Headquarters. Away to the right, "B" Company.

There were periodic stabs of small-arms fire, confused, some way off in various directions. Isolated elements of Hitler Youth, having crawled to ground under the barrage and stuck it out, were attempting to fight, often lying low to let the leading battalions pass over them in the corn, and bobbing up in the rear. There was a shout over in 8 Platoon. They had stumbled on a position. But the SS defenders, still stunned from the guns, had no time to collect themselves. Their hands were up. Someone was detached to escort them back. Others were stumbled upon: things in the corn that would never bob up again—and a thrill of revulsion when yet others were in all too familiar khaki.

We reached a hedge, and lined it. Beyond, an open grass field to be crossed. I kept the platoon halted. There were some pale objects in the ground by the opposite hedge, like human faces. I told a bren gunner to fire a few bursts over them, taking no chances, and watched for reactions. I raised my binoculars. Sick, I told the gunner to stop. We had been firing at our own dead.

We advanced again, and passed the dead some yards off. They lay on their backs in the long grass like winged birds, awkwardly propped on their haversacks.

Another field. Death-traps if a platoon were caught in enfilade. The usual thick hedges all round, and on the right a two-storied stone granary. There was a shot from somewhere. I despatched Corporal Nim's section to clear the granary. They worked their way round to it. Nim put a burst of sten bullets through the door. There was nothing there. We went forward again.

The Battalion completed their first bound and took up positions in the depression formed by the River Muc; only there was no river, not even a stream. It had dried up. Ahead the "Royals" were going into La Gaule supported by Churchill tanks. Further to the left the "Fusiliers"—the same battalion that Winston Churchill had commanded in 1916—and R.E. assault vehicles were in the outskirts of St Manvieu. Far to the right one of the Highland brigades was fighting for the Cheux high ground. There was a renewed intensity of artillery fire, but the noise was losing its novelty, and beginning to batter at the nerves like lost souls claiming their own. Uncannily the enemy seemed to know where we were, and his own shells came plunging over the Muc—mostly on "B" Company, where one of the subalterns was hit. He must have been the Battalion's first casualty.

"A" Company were in a clover field bounded by the inevitable hedgerows. In front more corn, waist high, sweeping up to a horizon. We dug in under grey clouds to the reverberations of guns, along the forward hedge. Two to a slit-trench. One man crouching, scanning that horizon of corn, while his companion dug for both. Somebody called out—

"There's a Jerry here." A dead one. Discovered in an angle of hedge, and the object of some macabre sightseeing expeditions. One heard comments—

"He's a good-looking bloke. . . ."

"He's good-looking, all right. . . ."

"Isn't he young! . . ."

There were whistles.

Drawn by their curiosity, I brushed through the thickets and made myself look. I had never seen anything dead before, except a cat in the gutter, or a bird: one had had barely time to register the half-hidden things in the corn that morning. I peered, and saw a pair of ankle boots. My eyes moved up the trouser leg and saw a hand. It was quite white. But I could not bring myself to look at the face that was apparently so striking.

"Look," I heard, from someone who had evidently taken the paybook off him—"he's only seventeen!" I suppose I shall always wonder what he looked like.

Then Gavin visited the platoon, looking for me.

"I want you to take out eight men with a bren, and patrol the Company front for snipers." He indicated the area to be covered. "Report when you're back."

I selected Duke's section complete, with Private Black on the gun. We set out through the rising corn and soon the company positions were unpleasantly far to the rear. We were alone, feeling anything but inconspicuous in the vast cornfield. If we crawled through the corn the task would take all day, so there was nothing for it but to walk forward, ready to drop to cover if fired on. We proceeded in arrowhead formation with myself in the middle, moving out several hundred yards until two hedges converged on a gap for farm carts. A good burst from a spandau could have finished the lot of us, and I sent two men ahead as scouts, to work by bounds. The rest followed, with Duke, large and bony, bringing up the rear as my substitute in case of accidents. We approached the hedge junction. The solitude was appalling. We crept into the left-hand hedge. Some kind of fly or insect kept snipping through the leaves and nettles, and madly one had to convince oneself they were not bullets fired with a silencer.

The scouts worked their way a sufficient distance beyond the gap without mishap. Every few moments they signalled back to me, tautly. I signalled a halt and went up to them, giving new directions. We retraced our steps to the gap, and worked along the other hedge. Then turned into the centre of the field again. I called in the scouts and together we all stalked through the middle of the field towards home again. The Company positions were now barely two hundred yards away. Suddenly we froze at a burst of fire from Black's bren gun, firing from his hip, and instantly an apparition rose screaming from the corn and rushed towards us, throwing itself at my feet. It was an SS.

He must have sensed I was the patrol leader. He may have been watching us. Quickly, a heavy Luger pistol, made in Belgium and fully loaded, was taken off him; but he was in no state for offensive action. By a neat bit of shooting Black had hit him, and his left shoulder was streaming with blood. He knelt at my feet clutching my knees, frantic with pain and terror.

"Don't shoot—don't shoot! Have pity! Don't shoot!"

He knew that much English.

We understood. To key up their resistance they had been told the British shot all prisoners. He now expected death in cold blood.

For a few speechless seconds we gazed at him. Black alone stood apart, a little upside down, surveying the results of his handiwork. For myself it was a strange experience to stare down at this Nazi clutching my legs and pleading for his life. One did not blame him for his terror. Nevertheless, he was of the "Herrenvolk". One felt no compassion.

We hoisted him to his feet. His helmet, covered by a canvas camouflage casing, had tumbled off, exposing a shock of blond hair. His eyes blue, his face under a several-day growth of fair down. By his paybook he was twenty. He would not walk unaided, so one of the patrol and I carried him, his arms over our shoulders.

"Don't shoot—oh, have pity," he still sobbed, beside himself from shock and his wound.

"No, we don't shoot," said a Jock.

We carried him into the Company positions, the centre of all eyes, and set him down like a trophy at Company Headquarters. He was quieter now. He looked at me. He would have killed me in that field. Impossible to tell what he thought now. A stretcher-bearer attended to his wound; two bullet-holes had torn the flesh. I had never seen Gavin so taken aback—he had sent us out on textbook routine, thinking no more of it.

"Well done, my boy," he said, incredulously. It was the acme of praise.

The prisoner was taken away.

CHAPTER EIGHT

THE WILDERNESS

THE battle developed. Guns battered unendingly, the echoes drumming and tumbling around the dismal horizons. Then the clouds burst. Sheets of rain fell, and to bleak news of casualties, including two of their company commanders killed, we were ordered to the support of the "Fusiliers" at St Manvieu.

We moved from our positions and set off across the steaming cornfields. A mile away St Manvieu church tower stood up among the trees. We made for it, and drenched by the downpour and the matted corn came to the fringes of the village.

Here carnage had been wrought. St Manvieu had been a strongpoint complete with a trench system and underground bunkers, and had been bitterly defended. The "Fusiliers" had gone in with Churchill "Crocodile" tanks that spewed flame, and other armoured assault vehicles designed to lob a type of small depth-charge. Afterwards, a strong counter-attack was launched at them up the road from Carpiquet, to the east, in which enemy from 21st Panzer Division made an appearance. But our guns had battered as fast as they could be loaded, and the "Fusiliers" still held St Manvieu. Now, as "A" Company arrived, there was an unhappy interlude; the village held in a spell, still burning, and ringed by snipers. The buildings smouldering. Others blackened husks. Here and there roofs and timber spasmodically subsiding into rubble. Gardens, kitchen plots and paddocks more or less a no-man's land. Walls everywhere bulged and split, pocked by shrapnel, and dirtily smudged wherever the flame-throwers had seared a path. And an awful suspense, and silence, and only the desultory crackling of flames, the random disturbance of something else collapsing, and the stray whip-crack of a rifle-shot across the open.

The Company went forward into the village. A number of dulled men in steel helmets wearing anti-gas capes against the rain were discovered in a captured German position; Scots Fusiliers, twenty-eight of them, and all that were left of a company that had crossed the start line that morning. The company commander was dead and a tired captain with handlebar moustaches was in command. I found myself sharing his trench. He had been reduced to a state of fatalism, and recited to me their losses in a strain of mournful satisfaction at the *fait accompli* of their day. Then came a new counter-attack scare. There was some confusion. "C" Company moved into the village. "A" Company were pulled back and harboured in a small copse on the west side of the place, and Gavin promptly disappeared on a reconnaissance. We saw no more of the "Fusiliers", but at a T-junction near the copse there were three of them dead under an angle of wall, with a 2-inch mortar already rusting. These, too, were propped on their haversacks, staring upwards. One wondered if all dead men reverted to their backs.

A road led eastwards down a slope and up past the church to the gentle ridge on which St Manvieu itself stood, and out through the village to the enemy, and Carpiquet. Another road came up past the copse from La Gaule and trickled on round to Norrey and Bretteville. At the T-junction now appeared the solitary figure of Colonel Ben. He approached the copse. He wanted Gavin. I was sent for. He was blunt and curt. Where was my Company Commander? Why had he left his Company?

"He's gone on a recce, sir."

Then where was Duncan?

"He's on a recce, too, sir." This was awful. But Ben was ruthless. I was the senior platoon commander.

"Then get your Company into defensive positions round the church; the SS are coming down that road." He pointed to the church and the road to Carpiquet.

"Yes, sir."

Ben stumped off. The Battalion at stake.

I called Alastair and Danny and gave platoon areas. The whole Company ran for it. We reached the church. A renewed deluge of rain came down. We started digging. Some of the youngsters were getting scared. A section of 7 Platoon were at work with their entrenching tools near a couple of abandoned farm-carts, their rifles beside them, facing up an open stretch of slope towards the village, and kept looking back at me. There was a ghastly sense of the unknown. Meanwhile Gavin must be found. I started up the slope past the churchyard for the village again. There was a mysterious increase of rifle-shots. I ran for my life, an image of one of the "Fusilier" majors who had been killed persisting at the back of my mind. He had instructed at the battle school in far-off days—a trim youthful figure and a gifted officer. But dead now. His qualities set at nought by a sniper in St Manvieu this hot June. And a heavy crack like a ringmaster's whip in a circus sounded above my skull, possibly coming from a loft in front. I leapt over a fence and dodged through some apple trees—and was among "C" Company. With no sign of Gavin.

However, before long he had reappeared at Company Headquarters. This was in a farm close to the corner of the churchyard and roughly in 7 Platoon's area. All the farm buildings had been hit. The yard was a slough of refuse and decay, and by the gate was a large iron cage. Inside, two huge black hounds were spread-eagled in death, their mouths crawling with flies and maggots; the wretched beasts, locked in and forsaken, the once savage guardians of their world. They capped the desolation, invoking mingled revulsion and pity. Gavin and Duncan had established themselves in a small stable filled with trusses of straw, with the wireless set and signallers. The remainder of Headquarters sheltered in adjacent stables.

We maintained a full stand-to, and evening was drawing on. Trenches were completed. 7 Platoon had a position inside the churchyard. This was a macabre sight. Down the centuries the forefathers of this crumbling Normandy village had lain here. Now the shell craters had ploughed up their resting-place. Their monuments rudely tilted and staggered by cordite; their vaults cracked. Some resurrection.

Platoon Headquarters were on the home side of the churchyard wall. Here my batman and I had a trench. We dug it deep and narrow directly under the wall. We found a heavy wooden plank and supported it across the trench mouth, leaving an aperture through which to fire. Meanwhile the enemy began shelling the T-junction, which was about a hundred yards away. We heard the shells whirring over the church tower; one heavy shell with utmost regularity every few seconds, viciously splattering the echoes, dropping with impressive accuracy and mercifully missing the church.

A message warned us to be prepared for rushes by infiltrating parties of enemy, and I fell to acute calculations of our distance from the corner of the churchyard wall. It would be each man for himself, no doubt, and they would certainly make for the farm buildings and Company Headquarters. But what of Jamie and me? Our trench was inconspicuous. What would we do if they rushed past it? Or they might trip over the headboard. Well, grenades ought to bounce off the top. . . .

The dusk deepened. Rifle fire from the village periodically flared up. We were in bewildering ignorance of what was happening. The rain dripped and trickled into our slits, and there had been no hot food since before dawn. The big shells banging away on the T-junction jarred us, while the faces of the three dead "Fusiliers" could still be seen there as pale blobs through the gloom and rain, motionless among the shells, with their ghastly whiteness. And this, and those savage crashes, and the great spread-eagled hounds, and the grim churchyard across the wall, evoked a dull weight of depression such as one never could have dreamed. All the elation of the morning had ebbed away. It seemed there was no hope or sanity left, but only this appalling unknown and unseen, in which life was so precious where all rotted, and where all was loneliness and rain. This was the war. It was bloody.

Then Seyton was killed. Seyton of "C" Company. Shot through the brain while going round his platoons in the village. This made a horrible impression on my mind. A sergeant fell with him—but the sergeant was shamming for dear life. When it grew darker he got up and away, leaving Seyton alone. Seyton who had smiled across the table over the portable during the 9 o'clock News on D-Day, three weeks ago. Now lying alone in that village. Seyton now white.

At length the situation came to its climax. The village was attacked, and "C" Company took the strain. Confusion seemed unending. In "A" Company we sat tight. Again and again the British guns spoke, as a field regiment rained shells into the dusk for prolonged minutes in a wide protective line. We saw the village once more, silhouetted on the ridge in its own lurid glow. And nobody budged, until gradually the whole shapeless action petered out. The big shells on the T-junction stopped. The rifle-shots died. Night came down on St Manvieu and its church, stabbed by the odd flicker of fire from some gaunt surviving roof, while men crouched in dripping gas capes still kept their watch. Finally the pitch blackness, thick silence, and the pelting of rain.

About midnight troops of the Wessex Division squelched up, in long single files, to relieve us. They, new to battle. We with our first day behind us.

Our own files squelched out.

Back through the melancholy rain-swept night we trudged. The way had been routed—Hat Route or Sun Route, we cared not which so long as it led us—and we merely followed the shielded signs dimly illuminated by hurricane lamps. Back along the muddy tracks over the battlefield. Back through the wilderness the way we had come. The gun areas had all moved up and innumerable emplacements and their impedimenta loomed at every stage through the dark. The rain was steady. In blackness we trod through Norrey again. By daylight, after a wet dreary night of incessant jerks and halts, we came to a village called Le Mesnil Patry where the 46th Highland Brigade attack had started.

Here we tramped through some of the "Fusiliers". They were halted at the roadside eating their breakfasts, having been pulled back before us in the night. A big dark husky major, familiar throughout the Brigade, stood watching us pass. At his side stood one of his subalterns, a beefy individual of spotty and rugged countenance whom I knew well by sight. Both were in gas capes; the major holding a sten gun, the subaltern with slung rifle. Two most solid Britons at war, who at least were still large as life. Mentally one clutched at these two, who gazed so stolidly at our approach, for some stability in a world of change. In their eyes something brooded which their friends and relatives at home would not have seen; otherwise they were reassuringly unmoved, and the same. The major indeed was to perform the almost unique feat of surviving the campaign unscratched. The fate of the subaltern I never knew. I never saw him again, or knew his name.

We marched up the way the Highland Brigade's assault had gone twenty-four hours earlier, into a new assembly area within a couple of miles of Cheux. The whole Battalion were harboured in one field, and here for a while we were to find comparative peace, except that the assault in this area had run into minefields: the Sappers were now doing their best to mark cleared lanes and danger zones, but one trod warily. We were also surrounded by a gun area, the guns spaced across the open and camouflaged by nets and foliage; their muzzles thrust at the one direction. Suddenly they all packed up, however, and moved to new sites from where they could administer a closer hammering.

Other drawbacks to the surroundings soon became apparent. For reasons of sanitation and morale the dead of both sides had to be got under ground as quickly as possible. I was placed in charge of the burial party. All Highlanders, the dead were scattered along the hedges round the field. The complete course of a platoon attack could be traced in detail. The platoon commander, a lieutenant, looking faintly surprised, a slight twist to his neck and not a mark but for some congealed stains where his battle-dress covered the kidneys. In a breast pocket a slab of chocolate as I had in mine, and a snapshot of his wedding a month earlier. Here, a corporal huddled over his sten gun, taken completely unawares. His face pudding-like, and the boiled sweets still in his pocket.

A corporal from "C" Company was among the burial party. "I know him! He was in my ward in hospital last Christmas— that bloke!" he exclaimed stupidly, his face a picture of ludicrous astonishment. With a big nose and a startled, lugubrious voice, a living corporal, blankly gaping at the dead one.

So we collected them and laid them side by side, and took the personal effects off them; most of which work, owing to the loathing of the Jocks to touch their own dead, fell upon the corporal and myself. A long shallow trench was dug. Others as they were found were brought to us, in ones and twos from the fields around, slung in groundsheets, by stray parties detailed for the purpose. They were deadweights, and the faces bored into you. One of them, very fair-skinned with blond hair, had a strange name ending in "-ski". He was unblemished except for a neat red hole in the centre of the forehead. His blue eyes stared before him in sightless amazement. A trouser-button was open and his genitals showed like wax. Another was a carrier driver whose vehicle had been hit by an anti-tank shell or gone up on a mine. His arms and a leg were in rough splints and his mouth was open, dried like leather and twisted as if in a last shout. Then came the surprised platoon commander, and we covered them over with earth. And there was trouble with a Padre who turned up from somewhere—a chubby fellow who tried to fob off a prayer-book on to me, expecting me to take the Burial Service. This was too much, and I left him holding the book.

Then there was difficulty over constructing crosses, but the corporal from "C" Company was ingenious and gathered sticks of wood. And in indelible pencil we scrawled upon pieces of paper stabbed through with a bayonet, in rough capitals, the number, rank and name of each. With the epitaph:

K.I.A.

26 JUNE 1944

In places the khaki and grey were intermixed, but there was a chalk pit, covered by trees and undergrowth, where all were German. They littered it like flies. Many must have been accounted for by artillery fire. Every yard there were bodies. The faint musty odour still comes back to one's nostrils in any weather. The first we came to had a pool of dark blood in the socket of his eye; we looked in his paybook and there was his photo, a good-looking youth, taken with a friend: the two young Nazis, smiling out at us in their prime, from Stuttgart or Dresden or somewhere. At one side of the pit was a dug-out, evidently a command post, with signal cable leading from it. Inside six of them were sandwiched, and a field telephone.

We dug another long trench and started filling it from one end, carting the rigid forms. They were the enemy, and we were able to view them more callously than the unnerving sight of our own. And they were so unutterably dead. There was no more life in them. The mysteries of the earth were as simple as that. A surge of emotion filled you and a conviction that life moved on elsewhere after death, and that life was the spirit. The discovery stimulated you, intoxicating, dull and heady, as we marked their graves with their upturned rifles.

Eventually I returned to the living, and sought out Gavin. "My God!—you're white," somebody said.

Apparently my party had been forgotten about. Compassion was taken on us and Mac the Adjutant sent out Sigbiörg, one of our Norwegians, with a fresh party, for the job was far from completed. Gavin took me to the jeep and dosed me with an extremely large rum.

The following day we were on the move once more, crossing the lateral highway Caen-Caumont at about 2 o'clock in the afternoon.

Meanwhile events ran high. The corps giving us flank protection had been held up, and this, with the minefields, had made the advance of the Highlanders drop far behind the opening barrage; but they had forced the Cheux high ground. The enemy had brought up his heavy Panzers, and Cheux, on the only front-rear road axis, had become the scene of appalling devastation, traffic jams, sniper scares, and lone vicious gun duels. The reserve brigade had been launched. One of the battalions had lost its Churchills, and ran into Panzers dug-in on its start line. Another spent a night surrounded. A bridgehead across the Odon had been seized, cut off and re-established. The Lowland Brigade had been ordered forward to widen the salient. In two days a wedge had been knocked five miles deep into the enemy line, and the charging Taurus armoured division was going through. . . . So was formed the Scottish Corridor.

We were now having a magnetic effect upon the German Army.

CHAPTER NINE

GAVIN'S HOUR

THE Battalion passed through Cheux. There was complete desolation. At a bend in our route the charred wrecks of tank and anti-tank gun confronted each other at a range of thirty yards: the savage epitome of this reeking strip of country to the Odon.

We went past pulsating laagers of Churchills and support guns down a littered finger of woodland that ended in an area called Le Haut du Bosq, where we took over from the Highland Light Infantry, who moved off for another attack. Towards evening "A" Company stole forward to occupy a further tree-line, and here we were mortared and shelled with uncanny precision and suffered our first casualties.

All night intermittent shelling groped for us. Next morning there was pandemonium, the sound of the guns welling to thunder again. The Division was obviously now fighting a defensive battle for its life.

We were shelled steadily, the enemy seeking to launch his infantry against our positions. The battle rolled across our front. A troop of three British cruiser tanks began a series of incredible evolutions in front of the Company trenches; racing to and fro to halt, swivel their grim closed-down turrets, and lace the hedges and thickets ahead with long, chattering bursts of Besa. Then away to another point to jerk to a stop and repeat the process, probing every conceivable approach, their main guns cocked and trained for armoured foe. Backwards and forwards they clattered, like great watchdogs, magnificently alert. We blessed them, watching fascinated from our parapets, and waited for the enemy. Seeing nothing and understanding less.

Soon pressure took the Brigade in flank, where the "Royals" became heavily engaged by tanks and SS infantry. The "Fusiliers" advanced to their support, and our own Battalion moved out in readiness to counter-attack. We plodded across more weary fields, harassed by random mortaring, not knowing where we were going. Alastair was hit, and evacuated. There were rumours of a hairbreadth escape of the Battalion "O" Group from a plunging "Eighty-eight" shell. "J. D." of "B" Company was wounded. In the middle of it all Gavin returned from Battalion and called the Company "O" Group.

Duncan was in temporary command of "C" Company, but the remainder of us collected in the shelter of some bank, our spirits oppressed by the day, and Gavin passed on to us a message that was to be quoted to all ranks. A message from Monty. We were, it appeared, his Nose. He had poked it outside the bridgehead. It was taking a knocking. Drawing the enemy's armoured reserves—exactly what he, Montgomery, had hoped for, and he was preparing a right hook elsewhere that would knock the enemy off his feet.

Gavin continued to enlighten us. The 15th Scottish were facing four Panzer divisions. The 12th SS had suffered enormous casualties, and had been joined successively by the 1st SS, 2nd SS and the 2nd Panzer Division.

The rest of the day battered on. Tanks charged the forward companies of the "Royals" at the dreadful moment when they were moving out of their trenches during a relief, but somehow the line held, and our counter-attack was not called upon. In the evening we moved forward again. . . . As we set off, one of the platoon comes to you, his rifle useless, the bolt jammed with mud. You snatch it and run to where a nearby group of rifles with British helmets tipped over them are marking rough graves, pull up a rifle for him, and kick open the rusting bolt action. A bullet is ejected from the breech, and the magazine is still loaded. You ram the bolt home again, and feeling profane, quickly make the changeover.

The Battalion now took over the Brigade front, the two other battalions echeloned in depth behind us. The same evening all our armour was withdrawn across the Odon, back from Hill 113 and Hill 112, back the way they had come and into reserve. The character of the battle had completely altered. All was defence now and dull attrition. We advanced to a château and dug in; on our right a small country road that was the boundary between the Corps of the White Knight and the next corps. There followed a day of ominous lull, with a sharp alert when two crack formations—9th SS and 10th SS Panzer Divisions, from the Russian Front—were identified from prisoners as having arrived opposite us.

The tale continues. A tale that General Eisenhower reported to the Combined Chiefs of Staff: "On 28th June, the British 8th Corps established a bridgehead . . . beyond the Odon river. . . . The greater part of eight armoured divisions was now flung into the battle by the enemy in a fruitless attempt to halt the advance and to cut the Allied corridor north of the river." And so this "green" division, whose men wore the Lion Rampant of Scotland upon their shoulders, withstood for its hour the brunt of the German Panzer strength in the West. Battalion after battalion rose to its crisis. The Cameronians, who fought the enemy hand-to-hand in a village down the road from our château; the Seaforths, who sustained three hundred casualties; the Gordons, with nearly two hundred missing. That night the enemy creeping into position for a dawn assault on the château, so close that the wireless warning to Battalion Headquarters from "C" Company could only be sent in whispers. And the next day, when the battle of the Haut du Bosq came to our Battalion. The day of which Lord Montgomery, in his book on the campaign, *Normandy to the Baltic*, wrote: "On 1st July the SS formations made their last and strongest attempt against the Second Army salient. 1st, 2nd, 9th, 10th and 12th SS Divisions formed up with their infantry and tanks and made repeated, though not simultaneous, attacks against our positions."

Every Unit has its story, and at reunion dinners men will reminisce. But to us, in that corner of the field held by "A" Company, the story was Gavin's.

Perhaps some idea has been gained of Gavin. He once quoted to me a saying of a brigadier he had served under—a brigadier who had evidently made an impression on him—which put the requirements of the good officer: "A harsh insistence on duty tempered by humanity," it went.

Which was something like Gavin.

Not that harsh really described him. At insistence on duty you felt a will of flint, but not harshness. Not the slave driver. Rather that failure to comply satisfactorily with duty caused his displeasure—and this cut. If he did make particular demands, it was on his officers, because he expected the most from them. With N.C.O.s to a lesser degree. While as for the Jocks, they knew that with Gavin if they tackled their job they were allowed to get on with it, and that if they did not they were punished: which was fair enough, and they liked him. They knew where they were with "The Major". . . . He was good with them. With them, where they were slow he grew patient, as with children. "If you do that when we go into battle," he used to say, in training, after some untoward mix-up, "you will get killed." Which again was fair enough, and they understood him.

An utter bachelor, he was so at home and confirmed in the sterner ways of a man's world. He was wedded, if the cliché will serve, to his profession. He was completely "Regimental". Most of us had a batman, Gavin had his "servant". Most of us went up to our rooms, or bedrooms. Gavin always went to his "quarters". We changed into "civvies" when on leave. Gavin into "plain clothes". And we subalterns in "A" Company— especially Alastair and myself, who had a complex about Gavin—used to envy the blunt assurance with which he addressed the sergeants by their names alone: "MacEwan", "Currie", yea, even "Macbain", without the prefix of their rank that to us was so necessary. And what finished us, the sergeants seemed flattered by it. . . . We had much innocent fun about his deliberate mannerisms. When we passed him in the street or gave him the Eyes Right at the head of our platoons, Gavin, we used to say, first took his pipe out of his mouth. Then he turned his head to study you. Then, we said, he made an appreciation of the situation. This accomplished, he would return your salute. Then he turned his head to the front again, replaced his pipe, and continued on his way—all on the line of march.

Gavin did not belong to our Regiment. He was seconded to us from another Scottish regiment where one felt his heart remained, and although he equipped himself with our service dress, an ancient balmoral that was not of our pattern firmly appeared at all times when he was in battle-dress.

A graduate of the Staff College, he had also instructed there, had held temporary rank as lieutenant-colonel and served as a brigade-major: he possessed all the right experience. With us he was renewing his acquaintance of troops for a command of his own. Yet one should not portray him as a type: the efficient professional.

"Gavin had the good sense to complete his education before making the Army his career," our Padre once observed. Coming a hot second to Gavin at *The Times* crossword, the Padre may have acknowledged him to be his one intellectual match in the Mess: but he meant that bypassing the normal peacetime route via Sandhurst, Gavin had chosen the university entry. Winchester and Cambridge had trained him. A soldier with brains.

I took to him the first moment I saw him. There was a remembered evening in the Mess when he was moved to cultivate Alastair and myself. In an agreeable mood he gathered us around his armchair to initiate us into some of the higher realms of military thought. Fixing the two of us with an amused eye, he proceeded to introduce us to Ludendorf's three maxims. An officer who is clever but lazy, quoth Gavin, should at once be given a high command. An officer who is clever and industrious should be placed on the Staff. And an officer— fixing us anew—who is industrious but is a fool should be allowed nowhere near troops. Whereupon Alastair and I went our ways agreed that Gavin clearly qualified for the first category. We also had a pretty shrewd suspicion that Gavin himself would have been the first to agree with us.

In fact, he had an amazing flair for delegating responsibility to others. A mound of paper matter would arrive into the "In" basket on his table in Company office. Out the lot went again: "C.S.M. for action"—"2 i/c for action"—"platoon commanders for action"—"C.Q.M.S. for action"—until it seemed that we ran the Company and that Gavin alone did nothing. . . . Especially platoon commanders. Three-quarters of Gavin's "Out" basket must have been addressed to us. We felt we did everything, and carried all the cans. But invariably he knew if action had been shelved, for nothing escaped him. And then one was demolished.

One always believed that if the next war came at the right time for him, he should be one of the generals; yet no achievement of his will surpass his subduing of Duncan when he took over "A" Company in 1943. I heard them late one night, down the passage outside my bedroom door. Duncan had obviously been won over, at the end of a long pow-wow, but was noisy with drink, pride going down behind a rearguard. Gavin was shushing him for the sake of decorum. "Little subalterns," he was remonstrating, "have long ears."

Inevitably one brackets them: they were, I suppose, the outstanding officers of my service. Duncan, tremendous at detail, the best organizer of them all. Arousing violent resentments, the sudden affections. . . . Gavin whom one respected. The ablest.

The preceding day had dragged by. Under the great hedgerows and in the orchard around the château, tired, unshaven men had completed their trenches. Within the Battalion area all anti-tank guns were sited for all-round defence. Three miles down the road past the château the Panzer concentrations and their satellite vehicles were being loaded up and fuelled by their crews, when out of a sultry sky 700 home-based Lancasters had thundered over the clouds and smitten them. All the khaki figures in the fields below had straightened up from their shovels, tilted their helmets off their brows, and smiled as if a tonic had been administered. And we had heard the brute heavy shocks and thuds as the great bombs did their work. . . . But at dawn on 1st July I was woken from uneasy sleep by the most devastating noise, and "Get your men standing-to—you ought to know better than that with an attack coming in," from Gavin, striding past my trench, rifle trailed and binoculars round his neck. He was passing through the platoons and peremptorily ordering them to their feet.

We had been keeping a 50 per cent stand-to, as we did every night, and as the bleary relief that had been sleeping stood to their arms alongside the other half the situation speedily became apparent to them. Whether by accident or design, the enemy was bringing his weight upon our positions at the inter-corps boundary. The Battalion were being heavily attacked.

The chaos of battle enveloped us. Noise raged, indescribable. It beat on our senses. It dulled us. It bludgeoned us. Never again did the enemy attain quite the intensity of shelling they put down against us here. And our own gunners answered. They were magnificent. Whether we could have stayed our ground but for our artillery is doubtful. Here was forged our bond with them. As attack after attack was mounted, the deadly 25-pounder gun-howitzers poured out their deluges. The road, and the château among its trees, were blanketed: the enemy so near that the gunners were bringing down their concentrations almost on top of their own infantry. "A" Company, on the Battalion's left, were precariously segregated from that inferno by the length of a field. More directly in front of us was the orchard that approached the château walls. This, too, was blasted by crash upon crash of shellfire and mortaring, under which crouched "B" Company, many of their trenches miraculously surviving amid the peppering of craters. The only way of getting across that orchard was to trust in your Maker and keep moving.

The noise roared on, overwhelming. Smoke, spinning shrapnel, listing trees and falling branches, and shuddering blast. To the soldier in his slit, impossible to cope. Just keep his head down and exist—until shouted at by his officer to stand up, because he cannot see to shoot from the bottom of his trench. And Gavin fought his battle. There were no heroic charges. No cheers for the Standard—we carried no Standards. There was no Death or Glory, not in this war, and at the end of it no decoration after Gavin's name. It was not even very spectacular. But he bestrode "A" Company, his influence and example standing out like a rock. Here visiting a platoon. There at a vantage point, with raised binoculars. Next with another platoon—and heaven help the man not alert at his post; and then somewhere else, calmly directing a smoke screen from the Company Headquarters mortar. At his feet a familiar Peter Pan figure who would have cheerfully turned his firing handle to Kingdom Come if "The Major" had so decreed: to wit Andrew—engaging the King's Enemies. Then—in answer to a frantic summons—back to dispel, patiently, the excitement of a platoon commander who had mistaken the posts of a fence, seen through the smoke and confusion, for advancing Germans. For, however it is with us, he must cope, and when all things have been done, it is finally upon the infantry company commander that the issue rests.

Time and again he had to make his way across the orchard to various Battalion "O" Groups. Then round with the evil

79

warning, delivered in usual matter-of-fact manner: "Warn your men the SS have been reported wearing British uniform." We had heard of them booby-trapping their dead. We had heard of them painting themselves white to assume death, then to arise and slay. But not of this. While here the Battalion mortar sergeant, a former stalwart of the rugger team, is decapitated by the awful fluke of a solid shot tank shell. This was the war. Vicious. Bestial. Insensate.

Then a single figure appeared, running towards us without a rifle. It stumbled through our positions; a Jock from some other company, and quite young. Some of us called to him, but he was out of his wits. He passed on, sobbing in gulps, the tears streaking the dirt and sweat on his face—making for he knew not where. And we saw two or three more figures in khaki moving back in disorder across the field, to disappear into a wood behind us. Then two men with a different badge on their shoulders arrived among us, who came from the battalion across the road, the left flank battalion of the other corps whose front had disintegrated. Quietly the refugees stayed to fight with us. . . . A little later a small column of some twenty men under an officer, who was Jansen, our other Norwegian, wended their way into our area, and threw themselves on to their backs among our trenches, staring apathetically upwards. They came from "C" Company—also from across the road—that had actually made the inter-corps junction. But "C" Company had been overrun. Tiger tanks had ground into their positions, and crouched on their great bellies stood machine-gunning our men in their trenches, and these were the survivors. And with all his crews knocked out, Gordon, the anti-tank officer, fought his last gun by himself until a direct hit smashed the gun and blew him out of the gun-pit. The enemy were infiltrating through the stricken flank to the rear, to surround us on three sides.

The knell of "O" Group fell across "A" Company, with a warning order to move. The "O" Group collected at Company

Headquarters but Gavin was over at the château with Colonel Ben, having sent back his runner with the stand-by. So we waited, and I still see the sergeant-major nursing dark, canny thoughts; and Gavin again reappeared from the orchard, imperturbable as ever.

Once more we clustered around him, flattened to the earth in an angle of hedge, while the vicious "Bong"—a half bark—of an "Eighty-eight" and the deadly rattle of a Tiger tank's machine-gun sounded in our ears. The bullets skimming the tops of the hedges above us. . . . "Tigers!". . . With their great black upright bulk that could give a Churchill about twenty tons, their vast tracks and the great barrel of their 88-millimetre gun, of all enemy engines they struck an especial chill into the imagination. And Gavin, sitting on the edge of his trench, spoke.

"A" Company, on the Brigade Commander's orders, would be prepared to counter-attack and restore the area of "C" Company. Meanwhile Colonel Ben was on the wireless, to the Brigadier.

"Aren't they Tigers there?" asked somebody.

They were. Apparently this was the point of Ben's wireless talk—that we afterwards learnt was not without its drama. However, as far as we were concerned, the Brigadier had willed: and so be it.

But Gavin had not yet been able to make a reconnaissance.

"I haven't been able to get across the road yet," he added, and for once a trace of worry had crept in. Then, noncommittal to the last about the Big Picture, he dismissed us. There was little reaction as the Company received the orders. To them, "The Major" had willed: and so be it. We moved off in single file down the hedgerow that led towards the road. Salvoes straddled us, there were cries, and men dropped. The stretcher-bearers clambered forward to get to those in front. Then there was a halt. A runner panted up to me. "The Company Commander wants you, sir." I went forward, past wounded men being carried back. Ahead of us, two or three hundred yards away, was a baleful sight. A curtain of shells tore and erupted along the line of the road. So involved had the battle become that British and German explosions were intermixed over the same ground. The rattle of machine-guns and the occasional strain of a revving engine, and far clink of tracks, seemed to come from all points of the compass. But by now one was used to bewilderment. I came up to Gavin at the head of the Company. He turned to me. He took his pipe out of his mouth.

"I'm going forward for a recce," he said, very deliberately. "If I don't come back," and there was a pause for it to sink home, "you take over the Company."

Then he replaced his pipe and walked steadily down the hedge to the hell at the bottom, as if going to Company office of a morning, waving his runner back so that two lives might not be imperilled. And that was the last I saw of Gavin. So I took over the Company.

He fell, dangerously wounded, under a harsh insistence on duty. Tempered by humanity. "When the Regimental Aid Post staff rushed out to pick him up," says the Battalion war history, "he told them to leave him and look after the many men who were coming back wounded from all directions." When they did get him back they thought he was finished. There were shrapnel wounds all down his forehead and chest. But he lived. It took him a year in hospital to recover. We heard that before he was hit he had been selected for a battalion.

Fortune on the battlefield hangs upon threads.

Colonel Ben in person strode the field, called off our attack, and directed us to new positions. Gradually the fight ebbed, and in the evening the "Fusiliers" carried out a sweep with tanks, and the crippled enemy withdrew. The Battalion had lost nearly 150 men in the day, and had not budged. "C" Company were less than a platoon. "B" Company had been partly wiped out. Eight officers had been lost since we first went into action.

There followed a vibrating night, but nothing happened, and no enemy were reported within 500 yards of us. And so ended the battle of the Scottish Corridor. Altogether the Lowland Brigade had lost 700 men in killed, wounded and missing, or something over a third of their bayonet strength. For a week we had not washed, shaved or taken our boots off. For six nights there had been barely any sleep. 15th Scottish Division had lost one-fifth of the total casualties they were to sustain from the whole campaign.

On the seventh day troops of the Welsh Division moved in to relieve us. We were withdrawn to Secqueville to rest.

CHAPTER TEN

HILL 113

I WAS certain I would get killed on Hill 113. Waiting to attack, you watched the "Nebelwerfer" rockets striking the start line with glowing phosphorus in the fading twilight, like giant cigarette-stubs falling from the sky; and knowing you were going to die, you confided an irrelevant desire to live on a farm and write books to the big shape of Sergeant MacEwan at your side.

The battle for Hill 113—we pronounced it One-One-Three—began with a night attack by the aid of "Monty's Moonlight", where vertical searchlight beams ringed the horizon behind the lines and reflected from the clouds a wan glimmer over the battlefield. The primary assault was delivered by our Brigade. The Luftwaffe came out. Two of the battalions lost their commanding officers. A bomb wiped out the brigade commander of 227 Highland Brigade and most of his command post. "A" Company went up Hill 113 with about 75 bayonets, and I think 32 men marched off it again.

Our Battalion were selected to take the top of the hill. We formed up on a start line which was partly behind the enemy lines, "A" and "C" Companies up, behind a concentration from 200 five-five inch gun-howitzers—someone said every "Five-five" in Second Army—and several hundreds of 25-pounders, and at 11.30pm we got up and walked into the middle of the German defences.

Today the Divisional Memorial, of Caen stone, stands at the tip of what once was the Corridor, facing across the valley of the Odon to Hill 113.

84

At Secqueville there were four days of rest. Duncan, emerging superbly from the Haut du Bosq with what was left of "C" Company and a Military Cross, returned to "A" Company and resumed his former command, and the clock curiously went back a year.

Returning to the fighting-line under an evening sky thundering with the R.A.F. thousand-bomber raid on Caen, we took over a holding role before the Odon. Day and night we heard the rumble of guns as Caen fell, but nothing much happened where we were except that Hill 113 overlooked us. The least movement drew shells and mortaring, so that we could only stir at night, and Duncan was carried away with a small piece of metal embedded in an indecent part of his person.

Soon we were back again in Secqueville, where there were three days of preparation for the assault on Hill 113. A fanatical officer called "Heid the ba' ", so named because of a tendency to stretch the head forward when walking, as if heading a football, here arrived from First Line Reinforcements to take over the Company, and when "Heid the ba' " went up for a company commander's recce, he took me with him.

We drove by jeep to the safety limit, then crossed the Odon on foot and climbed the Hill. The edge of this upland was now held by outposts of the Welsh Division, who were to provide the firm base for our assault. On closer inspection the Odon, surprisingly, proved to be little more than a stream, but its defile was steep and very broken and wooded, and obviously an effective tank obstacle had not the bridge been seized intact during the Corridor battle. As we climbed, the ground became littered with brewed-up tanks, and eventually a strip of blasted orchard ended at a calvary: beyond that a little ribbon of naked road led across the top of the Hill at right angles to our axis of attack, forming the start line. All was unpleasantly quiet. We reached the headquarters of a Welsh battalion in accordance with our instructions, and found the Adjutant, who uncurled from a dug-out and took us to an outpost from where we could get a view. The previous night he had conducted a young Frenchwoman to the same spot, and described to us how he had shaken her hand and turned back while she went on alone to cross the enemy lines on an intelligence mission. "I felt humble," said the Welsh Adjutant. "She was only a kid, but there are few of us with her guts."

The night before the attack the troops moved up, again through the smell of death at Cheux, along the now familiar route. "A" Company had to find a subaltern and three men to crawl about on the Hill in front of the enemy positions looking for mines, and Danny, poor devil, was detailed. All the next day we lay up in assembly areas among the woods and orchards before the Odon, where a timely parcel for Private Pratt provided 7 Platoon with quantities of cigarettes.

At dusk "O" Groups toiled up to reconnoitre the route to the start line and receive the final briefing. The symphony of the guns and the counter-shelling tuning up. The Welshmen settling down to take it. Then those final minutes when we fell in by the little road leading down to the Odon bridge, with the grandstand view of the "Moaning Minnies" bursting along the dim skyline where we must go.

To the roar of the guns we were off. Down through the valley and upwards to the shattering reverberations of the big "Five-fives" plastering the objectives, and the "crumps" of the counter-bombardment smashing down through the woods around us. Long columns of steel-helmeted shapes, hands gripping the bayonet frog on the belt of the shape in front, moving up the Hill. Fixed bayonets momentarily gleaming in the quick flicker of yet another explosion. Here and there men dropping, and a huddled form being carried downhill on a stretcher. Over our shoulders the night sky back to the sea was revealed, an amazing sight. There, snapped into life, the unwavering beams of "Monty's Moonlight". The inky fields riotously winking and sparkling with myriad gun-flashes, and over all, that spiteful thunder crashing on the Hill close above us.

It was estimated we should have to endure a five to ten minutes' halt on the start line. We emerged from the trees and wheeled right along the reverse slope, across a bleak flat ploughed field. A road bank became visible ahead: the start line. We shook into formation and lay down. Far in front, in direct line with us, sounded the cold-blooded chirps of a "Nebelwerfer" and the sparks of a stick of rockets streaking upwards into the night. We picked out their wailing across the sky above the din. There were one or two warning shouts of "Keep flat!" Closer came the wailing, crying over the sky for what seemed an eternity. "A" Company froze to the earth. Down it moaned. . . . down. . . . one's finger gripped and twisted the very soil. One's lips wrenched into a tight, silent "Please God, Please God."

The lot fell on 9 Platoon. There was a succession of sickening eruptions. A stunned silence. A few agonized, lonely cries. . . . "Stretcher-bearer!". . . And when, the next minute, the signal came for "A" Company, Danny and a handful of his men arose and marched forward.

We went in with bren guns firing tracer from the hip. The brens had been issued with tracer for morale effect against the enemy. We reached our first objectives to find them pulverized. The enemy foxholes were strewn with greatcoats, Wehrmacht caps, respirator containers, mess tins, even postcards and letters to the Fatherland; but grabbing their weapons and ammunition, the defenders had got out of it. Tools were snatched and we started to dig. A rain of shells whistled out of the night as the counter-shelling came down on us. As usual we dug in pairs, two to a slit trench. This time Tam MacEwan and the batman shared, while I shared with the runner. Suddenly something rushed for us. The four of us flung ourselves flat, our helmets pulled to our ears. There was a loud shock of blast and a screaming of fragments. For a moment none of us moved. Then the runner and I knelt up. The other two still lay. We thought they were dead. But after a few seconds they also got up: there was a fresh crater in front of their noses. We measured its distance from them: it was one yard from where their heads had been, and three yards from the runner and myself. None of us was scratched. For an instant we gazed at it, speechless, the four of us in the middle of the battle.

"My God!" I said.

"There must be a God, sir," said Sergeant MacEwan.

At the same time we were beset by enemy snipers infiltrating back between the companies. Many had hidden all the while in the abandoned tanks of the charging Taurus Division, where they were practically impregnable, and bullets came out of the darkness from bewildering directions. Here Private Pratt died over his shovel without a word, and most of the old faithfuls of the platoon became casualties.

And Private Black—perhaps the most faithful of them all. About fifty yards away a sniper in a knocked-out Sherman was troubling us. I got a bren gunner beside me, and one Private Henderson—uncomfortably far from Glasgow now—rattled bullets at a British tank until his magazines were empty. Then Black doubled over with his gun. Or as Black would have said, his "goon". For Black, who came into this world a month before I did, at Gretna Green, would tell you he came from "Coomberland". The gunner had got down beside me, and from shoulder to foot we were touching. At the first squeeze of his trigger the tell-tale tracer had streaked and struck the dim turret; there had been an immediate answering spark and a crack from the dark, and with a chopped yelp Black span to his feet, twisted over, and fell on his back in front of my face. I wildly bared his chest and listened for his heart, but could not hear it, and there was some blood, and somebody crawled over and put a field-dressing on him. All the time he lay silent with drooped eyelids; and nothing more could be done. Black had gone out of this world, again for the thing called Freedom. Such experiences taught us not to use tracer after all.

Everything was happening very quickly. A message came from "Heid the ba' ", who had a voice like a siren, which rasped above the commotion. I was to take a patrol. I took six men and we stalked through the long corn in a circle into the no-man's land between us and "C" Company, and around the same tank, where all was quiet. Warily we closed on the looming silhouette. A small puff of explosion cracked out of the corn at my feet. I fired three rounds rapid at it from the hip. A mistake; it was a German egg grenade thrown from the tank. The sniper was inside, still wakeful behind two or three inches of armour. The figure of Finlay, Commander of the Support Company, appeared in our positions. Would we like a gun? We would.

So he sent for an anti-tank gun, to put a round of solid shot through the thing.

CHAPTER ELEVEN

EVEN HE

THE enemy plainly had no intention of relinquishing the high ground between Odon and Orne. Hill 113 was defended by a Wehrmacht infantry division, and our prisoners all came from a Grenadier regiment. They fought hard to throw us back, but once more there was no rest for the Panzer Group West, whose stiffening influence was soon enough discerned. For three days and nights, playing their part in a wider battle, our companies on Hill 113 stood to their arms under incessant mortaring and shelling, and more than ten counter-attacks were beaten back by the Lowland Brigade. And we hung on to Hill 113 by our eyebrows.

The textbooks said never site yourself upon a captured objective, because the enemy will have you ranged. But textbooks sometimes have their limitations and sometimes you were lucky if you could site yourself anywhere. Thus Battalion Headquarters were plumb on the first objective taken by "A" Company, and as the enemy seemed to have discovered that here indeed was a battalion headquarters, it was being most heavily shelled at all hours. In fact, in many ways it was safer to be huddled down in your trench in the forward positions than to be anywhere in the neighbourhood of B.H.Q.

The journey back into this vicinity was a rather cat-like procedure. It entailed the usual walk-run, the periodic halts in order to listen, that agonizing pause before the swift shrill hiss of another "stonk" coming over; hollow-eyed, stubbly chinned men bolting for cover, the clatter of rifles, spades and trench headboards being knocked over—and your landing with a bump on top of somebody in a strange trench for momentary refuge. Then hard, heavy explosions and the trench shaking tiny rivulets of dislodged earth over you, the whirr of spinning metal, dust flying, and silence. Heads cautiously reappear and survey the latest damage. Here a scout car is in flames. What had been a motorbike is a heap of smouldering scrap metal. There the head of the Regimental Sergeant-Major, lord of the ammunition, peers from a hole in the ground under the belly of a parked carrier. From odd slits and bits of cover people emerge to continue their jobs. Nobody speaks. They were Headquarters personnel with tasks to be done and at their business of self-preservation. And the toll rose. The signal sergeant killed. The pipe-major killed. The C.S.M. of Headquarters Company, who marched in other times at the head of the massed bands, wounded. A direct hit on the Regimental Aid Post, the medical sergeant wounded, and a well-known, satanic corporal from Glasgow, who supplied "patter" at concerts, dead. The "Doc" alone unharmed. And further back, transport destroyed and casualties among the drivers.

The command post itself had been speedily excavated by an armoured bulldozer from the R.E. It was a large stout dug-out walled by a comforting thickness of earth; the roof shored-up with strong beams—in all a pretty neat job. Three steps led down to the entrance, and selecting the moment, one scuttled for it, arriving breathlessly but thankfully within.

There they all were, in the murk of the faint daylight from the sandbagged entrance and the light of a couple of hurricane lamps. Giles, now the Commanding Officer, for Colonel Ben had been severely wounded. Giles, at the start of the command that lasted him from here to the Cease Fire. So different from Ben. A face-veil round his neck as a scarf, loud of voice and harassed. One felt the thudding of the shells outside was more in the nature of a frightful bore for Giles, but for all the hunting and shooting demeanour that never left him, Giles probably worried a lot. He was, however, infected with the verve of "Bash on, Borderers," in all circumstances. Press ever on. And since he was possessed of an obstinacy amounting to an almost daunting single-mindedness, somehow, harassed but regardless, he invariably carried all before him, ending the campaign with a D.S.O. and Bar. . . . Giles was issuing directions—or rather shouting them—at Henry of "D" Company, who looked, and was, on his last legs. Henry looked as if he had forgotten what sleep had ever felt like. On the morning after the assault all contact had been lost with Henry's Company, for "D" Company, having unwittingly consolidated during the confusion of darkness in the middle of an enemy locality, had at dawn found themselves pinned to the ground and surrounded by Germans similarly entrenched. They were still in an extremely exposed position, on Point 113 itself, and Giles was wanting them to send out a fighting patrol, in broad daylight. Vainly Henry tried to get a word in edgeways and explain his doubt of ever seeing the patrol again: but Giles, too preoccupied for mercy, was waving all objections aside. . . . Then there was "Heid the ba' ". Quite quiet now. But with staring eye, ready for the least signal to hurl "A" Company at anything, anywhere. Beside him young Guy, who had gained a Military Cross at St Manvieu, raised through casualties to the command of "C" Company. Hugh, the I.O., marking both their maps with the latest situation. And Mac the Adjutant, seated at a small table in the centre. A wireless "19" set before him. Headphones clasped to his ears. Oblivious to everyone else, his voice raised penetratingly in wireless procedure, constantly passing information back to Brigade. Mac used to be signals officer before he became Adjutant. He could have talked wireless procedure in his sleep. Here in Normandy he very nearly did so. Finally, near the entrance, the Gunner Battery Commander, who always shared the command post. His two F.O.O.s out with the companies. His face pale and tired in the feeble daylight near the doorway. His eyes unhappy, absorbed in listening.

Restless. The nerves of this man, who time and again must have saved our lives with his guns and had wrought such slaughter, on edge under the shells of the enemy. And a second gunner wireless set, crackling in the corner, one or two gunner personnel, a corporal from the intelligence section and a few signallers and runners squatting about on the floor, completed the picture.

In a few moments there was another dose of shelling outside. A series of muffled thuds sounded unpleasantly close, as though the dug-out were being thumped by a vast fist. Blast smote the walls. The ceiling trembled and a few small stones fell. And no theatrical technique could quite recapture the atmosphere in that command post. Nobody quite stopped what they were doing, but involuntarily everyone listened. Speech flickered. Even Mac paused, in the middle of his headphones. Some instinctively reached for their steel helmets And it was then that I noticed the Padre.

He had been sitting quietly on the floor at the back, looking somewhat exhausted, with nothing in particular to do. But now his eyes were tightly shut and his clenched fists were shaking in a paroxysm above his head. The last thud went and he relaxed. Then another lot came down and again he flinched into the same attitude. After this time his eye met mine, and he held my gaze with a kind of defiance, and I quickly looked away. For it seemed a solemn thing, the Padre silently wrestling with his fear, alone at the back of the dug-out. A Man of God, old enough to be my father. And there was no shame in it.

CHAPTER TWELVE

THE TOP OF THE HILL

ON the enemy side of the Hill two villages quickly assumed the appearance of villages left behind in the Corridor. Both were down the forward slopes and in dead ground to us. To our left, under Hill 112, lay Esquay village, where 227 Highland Brigade with Churchills and Crocodiles advanced into scenes of astronomical confusion. Esquay became a shell-swept no-man's land; and in front of our own objectives on Hill 113 lay Evrecy village, which was held by the enemy in strength.

However, by dint of high effort during the night of the assault, the following dawn had found us dug in and consolidated, with the reassuring presence of Churchill tanks concentrated around B.H.Q. "A" Company had advanced to positions astride a small road just under the hill crest. Darkness distorted distances at the best of times, and we had dug in very compactly, daylight revealing the entire Company area to have a radius of only thirty or forty yards; but the strength was down through casualties, and everybody was at least under the direct control of "Heid the ba's" phenomenal voice. The trenches were in thick standing corn and a good deal of it had to be flattened. In front of us open fallow ground sloped gently upwards to a line of high crops that looked like maize, not more than a hundred yards away. This was the crest, and the road ran through our positions and disappeared into the maize and on to Evrecy.

The first sight to greet us at daylight was a formation of fighter planes swiftly circling the Hill at a low altitude. We counted seventeen of them, and as they seemed to be Spitfires we stood up in the trenches and heartily waved. Next time round a black cross was observed on their fuselages. They were Messerschmitts. They swooshed below the corntops and shot up a number of gun positions, rear echelons and ambulances in the Odon valley.

Later, a spot of lighter relief was caused by a tiny figure that arose from a skyline some 800 yards to our open flank. From a small ridge over there the ground fell away a little before sweeping right up to us in a great vista of corn. At first we thought it was an enemy patrol with a man carelessly showing himself, but the figure came straight for us, blatantly brushing its way through the corn with no effort at concealment and at intervals breaking into a trot, apparently alone.

As it neared our positions it started waving its arms about, and a solitary unarmed enemy soldier emerged, made a beeline for Company Headquarters, and sat himself down before the astonished countenance of the sergeant-major, covered in grins, waiting to be made a prisoner. His war was over. He proved not to be a German, but some luckless Roumanian conscripted into the Wehrmacht.

We were also treated to the curious spectacle of Colour-Sergeant Macbain, who came up with the rations (and never suffered from a not uncommon C.Q.M.S. tendency to become safely rooted in the rear echelons) crawling about, puce-faced, on Hill 113 delivering mail. Unfortunately he came up in the carrier, and evidently its noise had given the positions away. In the course of the day we were located, and the enemy crawled into the thick maize from where they could shoot down on us if we got out of our trenches. Soon we were completely pinned. A hundred paces separated our foremost trenches and the nearest Germans, and any vital errands had to be performed by taking a chance and wriggling on your stomach through the corn.

So we lurked in the corn and the Germans lurked in the maize above the fallow. Next morning, distributing the breakfasts was a particularly hazardous business, and packets of biscuits, cubes of dehydrated tea and tins of baked beans were tossed from trench to trench with all manner of weird contrivance.

Among others, both our stretcher-bearers were shot. One, a leathery fellow called Piper Ferguson, was lying on his own stretcher awaiting evacuation when he got shot again. While shortly a liaison patrol in broad daylight showed to some of us the sobering extent of the tank losses at the close of the Corridor battle. They were all over the broad back of the Hill, like a tank park.

A supporting squadron of Churchills clattered up the Hill towards us. A message from Battalion, screamed to the platoons by "Heid the ba' ", told us to keep down, and the Churchills, squatting behind us, proceeded to shoot streams of Besa fire over our heads. The corn was filled with the chatter of machine-guns and burning tracer, and we subsided to our trench floors pinned in ready-made graves. A lad in 9 Platoon flung his head up and died, and the tanks, working slowly forward, stood around our trenches still belting the skyline.

By now they were drawing a good deal of mortaring, which fell on us. Then "Eighty-eights" opened up from beyond the hill crest. A devastating high-velocity bombardment began: they were aiming at the tanks, but all their misses smacked among us, as one by one the Churchills were picked off by the invisible guns. One of them blew up alongside Company Headquarters and its ammunition caught fire; and all, ponderously, began to lumber into reverse as though ebbing away from us, still spitting defiance. Always in our coded wireless jargon the Churchills were referred to as "Big Friends," and now they were being overwhelmed.

The artillery put down a smoke screen to help them out, and we had a new element to contend with. The smoke screen, also, fell on us. There was a puff in the sky where the time-fuse ran out and a confusion of pops as the shells disintegrated to shoot forth triplets of smoke canisters, that curved their white fingers earthwards to thud among the trenches with frightening force. This seemed the signal for general commotion. There was more violent mortaring, shelling and counter-shelling. The whole performance filled an afternoon. In the end the nerves became saturated with it. One grew morally exhausted and beyond all fear. So one sat on, wedged in the corner of a slit-trench, boot to boot with the man opposite: fear run out. Past thought. Waiting for the noise to stop.

At last, towards evening, a blessed silence broke out. "A" Company rose stiffly to their feet and bleared at themselves once more. A peppering of craters covered our ground. There was one on my parapet. Astonished comparisons were made.

Even so, various individuals had to have it brought home to them that the war was still on. This meant that they had to be shouted at to wake up. For many of them, with the well-known phlegm of the British soldier, had in the end fallen asleep.

The Welsh Division were making an attack on Evrecy. Beforehand a Welsh carrier section appeared some distance behind our trenches on a reconnaissance sweep. Thinking we were Germans, they began to shoot at us with their bren guns. In vain Sergeant Halliday, out of his trench, waved his hands as he hopped back to ground—they hit him, and he died from a British bullet.

In the evening the attack went in. The Welshmen advanced in the last light, and a whole battalion came through us, echeloned out in platoons and companies. Everything was immediately blotted out by an appalling bank of smoke. We were standing-to as their firm base, but it was impossible to see more than a few yards, and the Welshmen, advancing over the crest, were swallowed in it. From the other side of the Hill we heard thumps and the rattle of small-arms fire. But something had gone dreadfully wrong. Soon they all came back again, reappearing out of the smoke in disordered parties and small groups and splinters of Units. The attack had failed.

Every officer among the forward companies had been hit, and a wounded major was brought into Company Headquarters. The battalion commander, himself a casualty, was rescued by a party in a carrier from B.H.Q.

When things were quietening down, more of us went out to get casualties back, keeping our eyes skinned for enemy following up. With stretcher-bearers I went up the road, and out there in the darkness stood beyond the hill crest a short way past the maize. It was the nearest any of us from "A" Company came to Evrecy. The stretcher-bearers were the reserves, with only one medical course to their credit, and there was a young Welshman breathing in dreadful gasps at the wayside. In our compassion we gave him water. It nearly killed him. He had been shot in the throat. Desperately we sat him upright in the crude hope that it would get the water down, and hoisted him on to the stretcher.

And when all was over the dim figures of the sergeant-major and Tam MacEwan could be seen digging Halliday's grave and burying him, in dogged silence, apart. He had been Tam's friend.

At first stray Germans, apparently unaware of our presence, would wander into our positions in the middle of the night. Once a small German patrol crept straight through Company Headquarters, where one of our men opened his eyes from what passed for sleep among us to find the incredulous face of a Teuton peering in over the top of his trench.

The second morning it was really touch and go.

It all began with a listening-post up in the maize, manned during the night by big Sergeant Duke and two men—the two badly shaken private soldiers flew back to me in the hour before the dawn, describing how voices had sounded out of the early morning mist and a large column of enemy soldiers, emerging like phantoms, had promptly taken the three of them prisoner. But Duke, recovering even as the head of the column was vanishing again into the vapours threw a grenade and his two men had bolted for it.

A moment later Duke himself got back and gave a more coherent account. The upshot being that a lot of Germans had probably arrived pretty close. "Heid the ba'" warned me to stand by with a reconnaissance patrol.

During the dawn stand-to he cancelled it but when we stood-down I was warned to get ready again.

Again he cancelled it. And we were just brewing up breakfast on the tommy cookers and Jamie was handing me my tea, when he changed his mind and told me to go ahead. I was rapidly becoming a nervous wreck, and took three men.

We ran for it across the fallow up to the maize, then dropped and crawled. We wriggled past a German body and I took the paybook off it. We crawled cautiously onwards, the three men at my heels. Raising my head, I saw a Panther tank on a shallow ridge beyond, its great gun-muzzle cocked in our direction. We kept flat to the maize. Then heard voices. They sounded Scottish. "I think they're 'D' Company," I whispered to the three behind me, for "D" Company were in that direction. We nearly stood up, but prudence prevailed and we crawled more rapidly towards them. The voices were plain now. I peeped again, near the edge of the maize, and there, for the first and only time in Normandy, had a panorama of the enemy at the wrong end of a rifle.

There must have been about two companies of them, busily digging trenches. The picks and shovels industriously rose and fell. About a hundred yards from us a sentry was turned partly in our direction. The whole lot were within a few hundred yards. We could have sniped them with ease, but it was not our job, and we crawled back with tremendous care, sprinted hard across the fallow, and I told "Heid the ba'" all about it.

Soon it seemed that our hour was at hand. On the heels of

my patrol there was activity in the maize. "Heid the ba'" yelled for a bren gunner to cover the road, so a one-time pigman from Renfrewshire answered "Sir!" from 7 Platoon and doubled out from his trench. We heard the crack of a bullet, and heard him die. His short shocked moans petered out in the stillness over the trench tops until there was silence. Then I was madly bounding out of my own trench to retrieve the gun, and jumping past the trench of the sergeant-major: a brisk "Well done, sir!—Well done, sir!" from the sergeant-major deep within, as though one were performing an athletic feat or walking a tightrope. But the sergeant-major and I were both afraid of dying, and I knew what he meant.

By this time there was a lot of movement in the maize, and we were clearly about to be attacked. "Heid the ba'" stood up in his trench and screamed for platoon commanders. Again I left the trench, but crawling now. Converging from the other side was Danny, and wriggling over the road a bear-like lance-sergeant called "Gib", who had been in the Company since the outbreak of war, and was now in charge of 8 Platoon. Then a bullet smacked into "Heid the ba's" parapet, kicking up a little spurt of earth at his back. As if pulled on the one string, the three platoon Commanders flinched, then resumed crawling. But "Heid the ba'" never even noticed. And the next moment an extraordinary sound was unloosed at us. Right along the line of the maize the enemy raised a war-cry. From end to end the shout resounded, and "A" Company fixed its bayonets, stood to its parapets, and prepared to resist.

Another shout went up. At the back of one's mind, confusedly, were the boys' books of childhood and their stories of dramatic bayonet charges of the other war. And naturally we had all been trained in the parry, thrust and butt stroke. And here we were, then: my platoon was the largest; we had fourteen men. There were six men left in 9 Platoon and eight men in 8 Platoon, and a few in Company Headquarters.

But it must be said that "Heid the ba'" now saved "A"

Company. He was a fanatic, of course. He stood up in his trench in full view, and yelled into his wireless for gunfire. His voice must have told every German for miles that here was a British company commander calling for artillery support, but he seemed to have a charmed life.

Everything happened rapidly. Back came the answer from the functionary known as "Shelldrake": "Then keep your heads down!"

In the nick of time came a violent outbreak of battering far to the rear. We ducked and the air was loaded with the sibilant screeching of shells that plunged and raked along the ghastly line of the maize, one or two shots exploding practically on top of us.

There was silence after that, and their stretcher-bearers were busy. It took them four hours to evacuate wounded and bury their dead.

The Battalion lost nine officers on Hill 113. A month earlier I had been halfway down the list of subalterns; now I was the senior one.

During the third day on the Hill I was sent to take over "B" Company, who had lost all their original officers. They were a few hundred yards in rear of "A" Company, and although they got their share of bombardment, from the point of view of ground contact with the enemy there was comparative freedom to breathe here. I found three subalterns fresh from replacements and no sergeant-major. And we then spent a fourth day on Hill 113.

This began reasonably quietly, and the enemy were thought to be pulling out. But the complexion of the day changed and from the afternoon onwards we underwent with increasing severity the worst bombardment of the lot. . . . We were due to be relieved that night. We prayed for the relief.

At two things the Germans were always adept. One was the almost mystifying precision with which they smelt out any sort of headquarters, and the other was their prescience over the matter of reliefs.

During a relief there was the inevitable moment when twice the normal number of men were in the one position, with first incoming and then outgoing troops exposed in the open, out of the trenches, when everything was twice as vulnerable. Accordingly, throughout this last afternoon, fierce spasms of mortaring and shelling were directed at all our companies, and in particular at Battalion Headquarters; and as darkness descended and all were primed for the relief, it was obvious that the enemy had somehow found out. They usually out-mortared us, and now the mortaring became especially heavy, and an abundance of Moaning Minnies sobbed over our braced lines.

I found the "B" Company subalterns to be under the impression that a relief more or less meant each man for himself. This impression had to be corrected; and I also received a blessing in the shape of a sergeant-major, sent from the support Company. But things were not helped when just before the relief, a wireless signal warned all companies that an enemy fighting patrol had penetrated the Battalion area and was probably sending back information. It was pitch-dark, and the enemy indeed seemed to know the very hour of the change-over. The incoming troops—a Scottish battalion for some peculiar reason in the Welsh Division—loomed out of the night on time, and plodded behind our guides into our trenches.

I handed over to my opposite company commander, busy on his wireless back to his battalion, then with my Headquarters was out of the trenches and back at the Company R.V. There was no sign of the rest of "B" Company.

Someone said the first two platoons had been there a minute ago, and it looked as though, contrary to orders, they had run for it. The sergeant-major volunteered to wait for the remainder, so leaving him I went in the direction of B.H.Q. looking for the vanished platoons, with most of my Company lost and the others being needlessly exposed because of the delay.

Nearing B.H.Q. another crop of shells came whispering out of the sky. Somebody shouted "Look out!" and there was a scramble in the blackness around me as men once more flung themselves for cover, but worried to death I turned my back wearily on the explosions. Empty-handed I came back to the R.V., where the sergeant-major was holding Headquarters and the third platoon, which at least had turned up. Then the "B" Company jeep driver presented himself before me from the chaotic dark.

All the jeeps were fitted with frames for evacuating stretcher cases: a jeep could take three stretchers, and the lightly wounded clung on anywhere. The "B" Company jeep had been sent back earlier with its cargo of casualties: now, with the perversion of this nightmare relief, it had reappeared. The driver was in a pitiful state:

"Sir—there's a Jerry patrol on the way to B.H.Q.; how can I get back?" He was trembling uncontrollably. The wounded were still on board.

I told him that if the whole German Army was behind us he had still got to get back, and to trust to his Red Cross flag. So he got to his wheel again.

We moved off, and were mortared all the way. The sergeant-major materialized at my side. Some men had been hit and had dropped out: had he better go back for them? I said we had better keep together and let the relieving battalion evacuate them. In a while he was beside me again, having promptly detailed a party, and gone back, and picked them up.

Company commanders had to report personally to the C.O. when their companies came through. Plodding past B.H.Q. I called a halt, and peered for the last time into the command post on Hill 113. There sat Giles in a tense atmosphere, and I reported the condition of "B" Company. He took it well, and I was told to write out a statement next day. Then, still under fire, we made our way down to the bottom without further

103

crisis, recrossed the Odon, passed the Battalion check point, and the nightmare was over.

Next day the Battalion were harboured in a field for rest. Here we were rudely taken by surprise and shelled by German heavy guns. We forsook the area and marched much further back for a quieter spot. This turned out to be in the middle of a British 7.2-inch howitzer area, and was attacked during the night by the Luftwaffe.

For the Hill 113 battle the Division had been transferred into the corps of General Ritchie, once Commander of the Eighth Army. It appeared that General Ritchie had thought this an excellent arrangement, and he now came round the battalions and told us so. All officers were lined up and introduced to him.

CHAPTER THIRTEEN

BEN

O N Hill 113 Ben had gone out in a carrier to look for the missing "D" Company. Our tanks had arrived, and while he was out of his carrier talking to the squadron commander, beside the leading tank, a mortar bomb exploded against it.

Ben, severely wounded and temporarily blinded in one eye, woke up in hospital to find himself in the next bed to the Colonel of the "Royals".

He had been the kind of commanding officer who never believed in taking cover. There were eight hundred men to be encouraged by his bearing in the face of the enemy: so Ben walked about in the open. He had been our Colonel for three years, and had one motto, one standard: A Hundred Per Cent. There was no argument. No alternative. And anyone not up to Ben's standard was out of Ben's Battalion. . . . On a famous occasion during one of the big exercises before the Second Front a new Padre was posted to us. It happened to be a Sunday morning, and the first duty this minister performed was to take the Field Service. Those of us who were elsewhere gathered that the new Padre had selected a somewhat tactless year of the Christian calendar in which to deliver his choice of sermon, and had said some rather outspoken things about the misfortune of our having to be in uniform. Ben, who attended the service, was so angered by what he heard and its possible impact on the troops that the man was out of the Battalion by lunchtime—never to be seen again in the 15th Scottish Division.

But for all that uncompromising demand in all things, the

Battalion had to respect him. He was just. A code of manners and human courtesy was the basis of his dealings with everyone, down to the youngest private. Ben was the fairest of men.

None, however, availed himself more firmly than he of that blunt manifestation of Army society—the privilege of rank. Ben was the Colonel; he acted like the Colonel; and whether in billets or in the field, he lived like the Colonel. He had a rugged philosophy that could scarcely be gainsaid: "Any fool can make himself uncomfortable." Which outlook, in fact, was applied throughout Ben's Battalion, and the result was that when they reached the shooting war they were good at finding a hole to go to, and often found things less exacting in physical discomfort than they had expected.

There is a memorable picture of Ben. It was when we were resting at Secqueville after the Corridor battle. Glowing messages had been flashing in from our higher commanders and Ben was reading out these flattering things and going over "lessons learnt" with his Battalion gathered round him in the middle of a field, when a German aeroplane swept out of the sky and began to dive-bomb an Ack-Ack battery in the adjoining field. The whole Battalion surged in a flood to the hedges, and rifles, brens, every weapon we had on us, were blazed into the air in a great state of excitement. The battery opened up too, but the plane made off unscathed. Then we noticed a lone figure standing precisely where it had been, in the centre of the field. It was Ben.

Ben's Battalion shuffled back to him with a growing sense of guilt until they were gathered round him once more, and Ben stood like stone, watching us. When the last man was back in place there fell the weightiest mass rebuke I had ever heard. In future the Battalion would not succumb to mass hysteria. In future officers and N.C.O.s would set an example, instead of running with the rest. There would be no such waste of ammunition again, at something we could not hope to hit, and the Battalion would not behave like a mob.

106

Yet in spite of the sternness, one recalls him with a smile. There was much about him to smile at, and much scope for the humour of Jocks. Jocks liked a personality. And Ben, Northern Irishman that he was, with a rich voice that could slip easily into a touch of a brogue, possessed a sense of humour of his own.

In appearance he was a short, fairly stocky man who used to stump about with a cromach—accentuated by his shortness into a rather formidable symbol, and had thin flat hair parted in the centre, greying at the sides, and rather a fierce little moustache. He had been commissioned in the Regiment a couple of years before I was born, and had come to our Battalion as Second-in-Command to a Peer of the Realm who was apt to address them on parade as "Bonny Blue-eyed Borderers." Then Ben, who never called them that under any circumstances, himself succeeded as Colonel.

He was not an accomplished product of the Staff College like Gavin, or the Colonel of the "Royals", but the posers of his calling were tackled as they arose, with massive application. "Difficulties are made to be overcome," was Ben's decree: and throughout Ben's Battalion it was so. He governed his Battalion by constant reiteration. His principles were uncomplicated, but immensely downright. He drove them home with the persistent force of a pile-driver until one could have screamed, and eventually not even the thickest skull was proof against them. His principles were three, in fact. Once he broadcast them over loudspeakers to the Battalion assembled in the dining-halls before dinner. And every Saturday morning of our lives there used to be a Battalion parade. And every Saturday morning of our lives Ben addressed his Battalion during the course of this parade. The address never varied. "Now, the object of this parade. . . . corporate act of discipline. . . . a clean soldier is a good soldier. . . ." And then they assailed our ears once more—the three principles. Ben's progeny. His foundations—and ours. The merciless trio from which there was no escape. Then off he stumped to the saluting-base, and his Battalion marched past the Eye of the Master. And in years to come, when the last survivor of Ben's Battalion quits this earth, somewhere there will be inscribed on his heart, ingrained deep and indelible: Physical Fitness, Mental Alertness, and Skill at Arms.

He specialized in saluting. There was nothing servile about saluting, Ben told his Battalion. Saluting was "a greeting between comrades-in-arms" dating from olden days when knights raised their vizors to one another. The Jocks, knowing full well what would happen to them if they were not feeling particularly comradely one morning, were invariably tickled by this, and especially so when Ben gave talks to the Companies about it, illustrating his point with an actual salute at his lectern. A wonderful salute with the hand cut away in true debonair style, the technique of which only Colonels and Generals were able to employ. And for several days soldiers would be seen imitating this swashbuckling salute in their dwellings—joyfully aware of the retribution if ever they dared to acknowledge legitimate recipients of the same in such a manner.

For a long time an outsize Regimental crest that was fixed to the bonnet of Ben's car whenever he was inside it burdened our lives. This appliance owed its inception to the fact that men were not being sufficiently alert to recognize whether Ben was riding in his car or not, and consequently were often failing to salute their Commanding Officer. So the crest, a fine piece of craftsmanship in polished metal, was wrought at Ben's decree by somebody in the transport lines. And the car drove about with it, whenever conveying him. Within, the Eye of the Master, waiting for someone not to salute him. The procedure then was simple. The car drew up with a screech. Doors banged. And out sprang a lustful Provost corporal who spent his life travelling as escort in the vehicle for this purpose—or on certain terrifying occasions, like a dragon, the Regimental Sergeant-Major himself—to take the name of the stupefied malefactor there and then on the spot. Later some luckless Company Commander would be icily informed from Orderly Room that his Company were not alert and that three of his men had failed to salute the Commanding Officer in his car that very morning. Due charges of Conduct to the Prejudice of Good Order and Military Discipline, and appropriate awards of C.B., would follow.

In the Mess he was charming. He had a great taste for Jane of the *Daily Mirror*, and also for his gin. Ben had a batman, a willowy man called Hume, and a standing joke among the irreverent of us was the rich, well-known voice booming down the corridors when we were dressing for dinner. "Hume! Hume!" it boomed. Came a swift patter of discreet feet. Then a throaty whisper: "Gin." And Hume weaved off to obey.

The miming of Ben was a matter of artistry to his subalterns. Especially Ben after dinner, over the port. High times on Guest Nights when Ben grew mellow. Now County Armagh would be recalled. Now the monocle would make its appearance. Much polishing went on with a handkerchief, and the monocle was raised with perilous uncertainty and adjusted to the Eye for perusal of the Pipe programme. He became immensely dignified and rather confidential, and apt to fix upon whichever officer happened to be nearest to him, with heart-to-heart conversation. On one breathtaking occasion he tripped against an armchair on his way home, and for a dreadful moment swayed on one foot, and nearly toppled over. Hands shot forward to catch him. But he regained equilibrium, and supported by his senior Company Commander was gently piloted to his car.

His peak moment, on bumper nights, was the "Mountains of Mourne." This was Ben's anthem, and the climax to many a fine time. Ben with monocle dangling, glass in hand, and once even standing on a sofa; and the whole Mess gathered before him. Ben in full brogue, verse by verse, and everybody, deep-throated, joining in with the chorus.

I suppose he saved the lives of many of us in "A" Company, that day at the Haut du Bosq. And I remember us pinned to a ditch on the destroyed flank, and Ben again, approaching us. Myself in the ditch at his feet:

"We're being sniped from over there, sir."

"Not very good shots, are they?" said Ben with a smile, still standing up. So I got up, and my men got up: there was renewed confidence. He was the Commanding Officer, four-square.

A request went up from his own Battalion Headquarters, when he was hit, that he should receive an immediate D.S.O. Somehow the Battalion, through the campaign, remained Ben's Battalion by nature. But perhaps the best comment is that to all ranks he was always just "Ben".

CHAPTER FOURTEEN

THE LAST HEDGE

THE rest of the Battle of Normandy rolled away before us, and to us Hill 113 was the turning-point. Moreover, thus far we were the Battalion that had marched out of Worthing; but from now on those of that Battalion were the "originals". There were many new faces. The turnover had begun.

There was a big intake of reinforcements. "A" Company's draft included a whole batch of Northern Irishmen, all Inniskillings and old soldiers home from Burma, who were to make their mark with us. I was promoted Captain and returned to the Company as Second-in-Command. "Heid the ba' " had taken over "B" Company, and with him went the redoubtable Macbain to be his sergeant-major. Duncan, a major now, was already out of hospital and again commanding "A" Company.

The night of 19th July had seen our relief on the Hill but even when the Welsh attack was recoiling in the fog before Evrecy we were, although we little knew it, on the eve of better things, and preceded by 2000 aircraft an Anglo-Canadian assault ploughed forward east of the Orne, beyond Caen. It came to a halt in a welter of rain and destruction, but the threat to Falaise had been achieved. By 23rd July the Canadian First Army was operational, and our letters home were headed "British Liberation Armies".

That day the Division moved eastwards to green, green pastures, and shrouded in secrecy we relieved the Americans near Caumont.

The Allied line had penetrated as far as Caumont within a

week of D-Day, and nothing much seemed to have happened down there ever since. We found a lovely land, steep and thickly hedged and bearing little trace of war, that resembled parts of Devon, and coming from the churned Odon battlefields it was like paradise. And here were the Americans.

Hitherto the Americans had been a kind of legend beyond the horizon, but here they were, very decidedly, with hearts as big as houses. They seemed thrilled to see us, and proudly showed their automatic rifles to groups of admiring Jocks. "A" Company fairly blinked when the particular company we relieved, burdened with more of the amenities of life than they could carry, enthusiastically handed over the whole of their surplus supplies to us before marching out. This windfall covered the entire floor of a farmhouse attic knee-deep. We discovered enough lavatory paper for a brigade, quantities of excellent tobacco and cigarettes, candy, various tinned foods, and cigars. In all, the departed host had been quite the most refreshing thing that had happened to us in Normandy.

The Battalion were in a reserve position here. The situation still brooded: a patrol or two was sent out and an American support company left in the vicinity got mortared a bit, and one wondered if both sides would have preserved the wary *status quo* indefinitely in this summer stealth at Caumont if left to their own devices. But soon the spell was shattered, when behind carpet bombing the American First Army drove for their break-out to the distant Loire. Another week, and General Patton's Third Army was in action.

Meanwhile we had moved into Caumont itself. Here Duncan and I dwelt in the cellar of a shambled house by candlelight, among a wild confusion of maps, tins, rifles, biscuits, other rations and Company Headquarters equipment. Here Duncan got edgy: however hard we tried, he complained, no two people could turn a place into a pigsty quicker than we could. The same night the Luftwaffe, suspicious, intruded again. We were in the cellar listening to the drone of the planes when Duncan remarked: "I think we're going to be bombed," rather as though one were expecting rain. The same second a large bomb dropped near the doorway, blew down the blackout curtain, snuffed the candles out, and spoilt an anti-tank gun that had been sited outside.

Next day, 30th July, the weight of Second Army was suddenly shifted. The awful bombers now thundered over Caumont. The 15th Scottish, green no more, attacked. To the left an army corps went for Villers Bocage. A couple of armoured divisions were waiting to exploit—and now, at last, we were moving. It was an incredible sensation. Six miles were covered in one day, all the objectives were reached, and the armour was pouring ahead. It was a break-out.

Events swept on, and our Battalion were ordered up, with enemy armour converging on a gap in the front at a high sullen feature called Bois de l'Homme, crossed by the main road from Villers Bocage to Avranches. We attacked it, and gained the woods at the top to find several knocked-out Panther tanks, large numbers of enemy dead—most of them extraordinarily young—and the moaning of wounded among the trees. The Battalion had brought down the fire of eight field regiments of artillery and R.A.F. rocket-firing Typhoons to get into the Bois de l'Homme, and this, it turned out, had caught a battalion of the 1st Panzer Division in the act of forming up to counter-attack, and had decimated them. But it seemed we were hardened by this time to any sight. We trod among the bodies of those blond boys with hardly a thought, and I was sent on a special patrol down into the woods on the other side to see if there were any live ones left. There were only the dead.

We plunged through the *bocage* into the wilderness of the Normandy Highlands and the wooded tangle of country between Beny Bocage and Mount Pinçon; now ferried forward on the backs of Churchills, now detached under command of the Guards Armoured Division. Waded in darkness through more woods to a burning village occupied by the Guards, with

113

the threat of more enemy tanks coming up. Stood a-top a high feature at night, with an attack planned for dawn down below: and here Duncan sent me ahead to reconnoitre the Company forming-up place at the bottom. While I was making my way down the side of a large shoulder with a runner there loomed out of the darkness another warrior, coming up the hill towards me, and also accompanied by an escort. So I halted. The other halted. We were about twenty paces apart. It was an impasse.

"Who goes there?" I demanded, raising my rifle.

The other raised his.

"Password or I shoot," came an even English voice through clenched teeth out of the pitch night. It was Henry of "D" Company, taking no chances.

I gave my name and started forward in some relief.

"If you come any closer I will shoot you," smote my ears. And again Henry asked for the password. I stopped, chagrined. It could only happen with Henry. But we could not stay there all night pointing our rifles at each other: lamely I gave the password.

At dawn we attacked over a cliff, eleven or twelve miles south of Caumont. Toiled under a blistering August sky the interminable length of a wild high ridge, and that night attacked again—a forsaken spot called La Motte, lost to most maps. We were growing somewhat jaded now. We had been in the battle-line or on ceaseless operational moves for nearly two weeks, and the enemy was recovering his balance. Since the Bois de l'Homme resistance had been negligible, but familiar opponents were hastening to our front, and 9th SS and 10th SS Panzer Divisions were bumped. All that hot day along the ridge they had the forward slopes under observation and mortar fire, and below us the Welsh Guards were engaged by Tiger tanks. At nightfall the whole crest stood burning: hayricks, farmsteads and undergrowth—all glared indiscriminately. A profusion of "Nebelwerfers" wailed over the scene, and "A" Company were unable to capture their objective for the simple reason that it was on fire.

At this time the big German counter-stroke developed against the Americans at Avranches. While eastwards the bombers were at work again, as the Canadian First Army set out down the terrible road from Caen to Falaise.

On our own front the advance had been held up, but the following day the Lowland Brigade moved up once more, with a full array of armour and "Funnies". We assaulted Estry.

Estry stood on rising ground surrounded by very thick country, with a visibility of rarely more than a few hundred yards. We failed to capture the village itself, and in "A" Company we never saw the village at all.

As the assault went in we discovered that the German outposts, perched among the hedges and cross lanes above us, must have watched all our reconnaissance parties clambering about in the early mist before the attack. It was quite an eye-opener. You could see freshly cracked eggshells scattered over their weapon slits and bits of black bread everywhere, and you saw incidentally how they could have shot us. However, when our guns opened fire they had evidently been withdrawn.

Casualties rose steeply again. Severe mortaring fell on us as the companies moved in, and marshy ground held up the tanks. "Eighty-eights", spandaus, bazookas and riflemen opened up from close cover. The "Fusiliers", on our left, were brought to a standstill and lost their colonel. Our leading companies, struggling for the village, were met by heavy fire from Panther tanks. The Churchills were unable to clear the place, and by evening "C" Company were in one half of the place and the Germans remained in the other. By now a counter-attack had driven the "Fusiliers" back, while Henry's Company, having penetrated furthest of all, was in danger of annihilation. But their withdrawal was sanctioned by a new Brigadier, who sorrowed at loss of life, and "D" Company lived to fight another day. A few nights later Henry went out to test the alertness of his sentries, when unknown to him a warning had gone round that a German patrol was also out. . . . He was the last of our original Company Commanders.

So there we were. Poised. Neither side quite able to force a decision on the other. The "Royals" waiting behind us to counter-attack if we got pushed back. And the curious thing was that the German resistance in Normandy was supposed to be crumbling. A hush prevailed, broken by the restless thumps of mortaring or a random outbreak of shells battering into the enemy lines. Away on the horizon towards Falaise the constant rumbling of guns distantly shivered cloudless, hazy blue skies. And the enemy, appearing from behind a hedge, snaffled one of our officers and made off with him, captive. While the hot sun climbed through August.

There was now no movement at all except for some sergeant visiting his posts, or a small carrying party toiling up in the shade of a hedgerow with jerrycans of fresh water, for the canny brewing of tea in the depths of the trenches. And we lay quiet, as the Germans lay quiet. Watching, as they watched. It was difficult to realize that those calm treetops so close in front were German tree-tops, with German helmets under them, lying up for us over German sights; but perhaps one of our patrols would probe forward down the hedgerows, causing their spandaus to open up from several directions, and the bullets snipped over the corn. These weapons, with their incredible rate of fire, were blazed off at intervals, day and night, on fixed lines up the hedges and over our heads.

And so, in dusty weapon slits sunk close to these hedges, among the laden, unharvested corn, slashed by the tank tracks and pitted with craters, dwelt that remarkable being, the British soldier. In his shirt-sleeves because of the heat, his tunic rolled under his haversack straps, his sweaty steel helmet discarded, although it should be on his head. Dourly cleaning the dust from his rifle or oiling the bolt action, or thinking of home in the brooding silences; or writing a few unbelievably non-committal lines to his family on the back of a mess tin that still bears traces of the last stew; or perhaps reading that crumpled backnumber from Kirkcudbright or somewhere. Or just sleeping. Two rifles mounted on his parapet for instant use, and his mate standing-to at one of them, stolidly gazing up the hedgerow to those German trees.

Three weeks after the move to Caumont had taken place, we were relieved. The relieving troops, hearing a strange silence, discovered the place to be empty. The armour took over.

By now the entire Big Picture was in flames. The Americans were wheeling up from the south, the Canadians gaining from the north, and the trap was closing. The whole sullen front gave before Second Army in the centre.

A few hours' laager in the orchards north of Estry, and we were off again. Back eastwards in convoy, the Division on the move. Back across the eerie empty battlefields between Odon and Orne; back over those twin monuments to sacrifice, Hills 113 and 112, along what only a week before had been the German side; and so into laager among the wasps and mosquitoes near the junction of the two fatal rivers, south of Caen.

A couple of days here, then on again. Through the shambles of Thury Harcourt, and another halt. An enormous convoy crammed with dishevelled, dusty Wehrmacht prisoners rolls in the opposite direction: "The Bastards!" wrenches out my truck driver with a sudden rush of feeling; while a great bearded Frenchman, like a ferocious dog, stands alone in the desolation of a village square, shaking his fist at the vast P.O.W. convoy and yelling after them as though his heart would break: "Kaput! . . . Kaput! . . ."

Then our advance party comes to another smashed village, abandoned to a gruesome population of German dead: there is a warning that everything is booby-trapped, and we cannot enter.

But the 15th Scottish were being "pinched out" of the battle, and there was no space for us in the final act. From Montgomery came the comment: "The situation is most interesting."

The massacre was on, at Falaise.

They called it the "killing ground". Too late the vanguards of the Fifteenth Army, immobilized in the Pas de Calais for fear of another invasion there, hurried southwards. The German armies in Normandy were defeated. The battle of the bridgehead was won. . . . The skies opened.

To those of us who had survived it, to feel, to behold a tree, to breathe God's air—to be alive—was a marvellous and miraculous thing. We passed through Falaise, and out of the sickening fields of Calvados, through the gathering tumult of a wild-eyed France, to the Seine.

CHAPTER FIFTEEN

THE SOUL OF NORMANDY

THE other side of Falaise a small party of us, selected for forty-eight hours at the White Knight Corps rest-camp, which had now opened behind on the beaches, dropped from the Battalion and set off in the opposite direction in a lone liberty truck. Quickly we skirted the aftermath of the Falaise pocket. All round a countryside that had for long been the rear of the German lines at Caen and on the Odon and Orne battlefronts were the cemeteries of SS killed in the earlier fighting. The rows of wooden Iron Crosses marking the graves made a violent impression. Their thick black bordering and bold black gothic inscriptions; and on each the "SS" streaked like lightning, with the crude, defiant valediction: "Meine Ehre heisst Treue!" At the head of each cemetery a huge Iron Cross simply proclaimed:

SS
UNSERE EHRE HEISST TREUE!

Further back we travelled, leaving them behind, brutal, pagan, and oddly sad as we traversed in an afternoon the span of the Battle of Normandy. Straight up the shambled highway through the bomb-ploughed wilderness from Falaise to Caen, sprinkled with graves all the way. To Caen itself, impassable for the destruction, with a detour cleared by bulldozers around the outskirts, among the mountains of ruin and enormous bomb-craters plastered so close they almost overlapped. Back through the leisurely turmoil of the myriads in uniform that seemed to dwell like ants behind the fighting line: Lines of Communication, Rear Bases, Main Bases, Depots, Dumps and

Roadheads of all descriptions with all their minions, until the actual fighting-troops resembled some remote minority away at the tip of this fabulous supply system: and so to the rest-camp on the seashore. And here, in the quietness of evening, with the flotsam of derelict landing craft piled offshore and the pierced anti-tank scaffolding and gaping façades of the buildings along the waterfront, I paced the sands with the Adjutant of our 1st Battalion which had come ashore in the 6th of June landings near this spot; and he, also having a spell at the rest-camp, described the happenings of that day. While local girls flirted with soldiery from installations along the beach, and everything seemed on the backwash; on the ebb-tide; already receding into the limbo of history.

For the soul of Normandy was in the gusts of the guns. It was in the desperate stench of cattle, where whole acres of the poor brutes, uncomprehendingly slaughtered in the barrages, lay stiffened and swollen to grotesque proportions, with their innards running out; putrefying the air and bringing plagues of flies. It was in the Haut du Bosq, where those forward companies had been charged by Panzers; where we found men torn apart by tank tracks and crushed into every mockery of the human form. It was in a fear that you could hardly believe. In the damp odour of the dead. The frightening corn. A woman's corpse half-buried in the rubble of a cottage, and the dazed little strings of civilians, with their bundles, fleeing towards Caumont, and the droning bombers like legions of ogres, black in the midsummer skies. There was no hope in it, only dread, and the cold inhumanity of battle.

And a Jock, who whenever we went back out of the line whistled Chabrier's "Spanish Rhapsody", and the soul of Normandy was in the tune as he passed. . . .

And the enemy.

They had "Gott Mit Uns" on their belts and met us with a sneer. With sentimental verses and coloured prints of flowers in their breast pockets, among postcards of guns and tanks.

With little cardboard crosses and tiny wayside plants pressed in the pages of their paybooks, and without humour, as humour was known among us, in their faces. A harshness, something mirthless, in the stamp of them, that remained even in death. With Goethe and the Gestapo, Beethoven and Belsen, flowers and the gas-ovens behind, the sentimentality and the tortures all written in them, and with tight-lipped, bitter verve they fought. . . . Above all, we saw the dark face of the Waffen SS And this we broke, in Normandy.

The summer recedes. The soul of Normandy hovered in the cloud of flies over the intestines of two German corpses, off the high road near Beny Bocage. They had been shot into human tripe by a tank. It showed in a dirty old peasant in a broken-down cottage on the way to Estry, who bared his chest to me and revealed a Cross of Lorraine on a chain round his neck, and bade me drink to France with him from a foul bottle of Calvados. It was with you when marching out of the Scottish Corridor like a man who had been condemned to the tomb and reprieved. And with the summer goes a last glimpse: that of a particular officer who once belonged to our Mess, dwelling among us like a small gale. For he was cheery and penetrating of voice to an extent that maddened, and people turned their collars up when they saw him approach, and yet everyone liked him. And coming from the Scottish borderland he requested, when we made wills at Worthing, that if he died a clump of trees should be planted to his memory among his home hills.

When we sailed he went back to First Line Reinforcements, only in due course he was diverted to the 1st Battalion. We later heard he was found in Caen without a mark on him, quite dead from blast. Aged rather a young twenty-four. . . . The summer was done.

INTERLUDE FOR TEN

WE made an assault crossing of the Seine at a beautiful loop of the river near Louviers, where a fine wooded escarpment crowned the north bank. In most places opposition was negligible, and the Battalion's only casualty was "B" Company's colour-sergeant following up afterwards with rations, whose boat capsized. Being unable to swim, he was drowned in the placid waters. This shocked us far more than if there had been the usual battle casualties.

The flux of the Army from the Pas de Calais had added to the enemy's disorder. Quantities of retreating Germans had struggled back across the Seine, but for miles the roads out of Calvados had been ghastly with smashed equipment and motor convoys blown up by the R.A.F. Frenchmen had been seen marching out platoons of prisoners to bury the beasts of the enemy's horse transport, and to fill in bomb craters. Paris was free. The Allied landings in the South of France had been effected.

The river crossed, we pushed northwards from our bridgeheads through a rolling agricultural countryside studded with dense forests. Here for the first time we encountered the Maquis, and small groups of them would be passed at the roadside remorselessly ferreting out hapless enemy remnants. Within a few miles we reached a small farming village where we went into quasi-operational laager. According to the excited inhabitants the Germans had melted away about three hours earlier, at dawn that morning. Soon a German officer and two orderlies, unaware of the change, drove in a car clean up the main street—to be greeted by a hail of bullets through the windscreen and promptly captured.

"A" Company Headquarters took up residence in a new

and rather glaring villa where we were instantly welcomed by the typically mysterious ramifications of a French family. They were apparently only caretaking for the owners—whom we confusedly understood to be collaborators and in Paris, or prison, or somewhere. There was Monsieur, permanently wearing a beret, and very rustic; Madame, a few inexplicable cuts above him; a small boy, who looked quite like Monsieur and also lived in a beret; a smaller girl who was the little boy's sister; an adult girl; and one or two aged countryfolk of various sexes who emerged painstakingly from the cellar. The departure of "Les Boches" that morning was enthusiastically described to us. "Bandits! Bandits!" they said, and their hatred was very real. But it was Monsieur who had the most to say. Monsieur had a story to tell, and he told it several times. "Ecoutez!" said Monsieur, catching hold of our tunics. "Un SS ici! . . . dans la cuisine! . . . . doucement!" he said, "un SS—et moi;" here he let go of us to tap his chest with utmost significance. "Dans la cuisine. . . . Egorgé!". . . Monsieur, it appeared, had sat an SS trooper down at the kitchen table, obediently served him with a meal, and slit his throat with the carving-knife.

As for the little girl, she became quite my girl friend. She was ten, and the prettiest little creature. She would follow me about and periodically wrap her arms around my waist, and while we were there I had my birthday: on the day I heard my name called down the street and there she was, running after me with a bunch of flowers. These were pressed into my hands "pour vos vingt-deux ans!"

We spent several days there, and were soon left high and dry without any operational role. Other troops and the armoured divisions were streaming up France, and with transport strained to capacity ferrying the armies northwards we could merely wait until sent for, and in the meantime get reorganized and cleaned up. The villa now became an officers' billet, and the highlight of these few days was a party we held there one evening. A grand party.

It started in high spirits. Duncan presided as host, assisted by Scottie, the Pioneer officer replacement, who organized the food with such professional aplomb that one strongly suspected his vocation lay in the hotel industry. Then the others. Two old faces who had been lost and restored to us: Gordon, recovered from his wound at the Haut du Bosq and returned to the anti-tanks, and the rather debonair Denis from whom I had taken over "B" Company when he was hit on Hill 113. Then our king-pin—Mac the Adjutant. That doughty dialectician, the Padre; but quiet unless provoked, and a little grey. Another old face in Fred the Quartermaster: a face that shone with bonhomie in which a kindly pair of very dark brown eyes brightly twinkled; yet endowed by twenty-four years' service with wits as sharp as needles, was Fred. And a further old face in Percy of Headquarters Company, with the mild turn of irony. He had a baby about this time, and telegrams went backwards and forwards to a spouse in Edinburgh. Finally myself, and our new subaltern to "A" Company, Colin, a soft-spoken Scot who had arrived after Estry—where Danny was hit. And so here we were assembled for our party. Three wore the ribbon of the Military Cross, and seated round the table were eight of the twelve officers still with the Battalion who had been present when we landed.

But there were no reflections. We were living in the present, and grateful for it. There was an air of abandon over everybody. Normandy was over. And was not Fred tomorrow doing an unheard of thing in going forty miles ahead of the Battalion— to Amiens—to the roadhead for rations? Why, there was news that the armour had entered Arras! Life was tremendous.

The fare, although organized by Scottie, had been initially procured by the useful combination of Fred and Madame. And the first course—an omelette—was hailed with glad cries. It was a monster omelette. No less than twenty-four eggs had been spirited by Madame into this creation, to be strictly portioned out by Scottie and washed down with draught cider.

124

Then the door opened again and Madame, thrilled to the core, bore in two roast geese, followed by a gallon container of potatoes, a large bowl of salad, and a thick salad cream concocted as only Madame knew how. All this was greeted with yells of "Ma foi!"—"C'est magnifique!" and "Très beaucoup!—très beaucoup!" in answer to Madame's anxious inquiries. There was some rivalry as to who should carve these birds, the various claimants loudly voicing their qualifications. Finally Gordon got control of the knife, and after a generous helping had been sent out to Madame, they went the way of all good goose-flesh. Conversation became facetiously flavoured the French way—

"Pass the cidre. . . ."

"Have some salade. . . ."

And people informed one another that in this house there were two "filles" and a "garçon".

Next came Army treacle duff. This had been Fred's province, and Army treacle duff was quite good, really. Then red wine was passed round, and after muttered consultations at the top of the table Duncan rose, glass in hand, and advanced to the kitchen door. Then with a fine flourish he opened the door, stepped inside, and presented Madame with a glass of whisky. With his own glass upraised he proclaimed: "Madame—Vive la France!" It involved a substantial deployment of his French vocabulary, but was entirely adequate for the occasion. At once the remainder of us in the dining-room broke into the "Marseillaise". Nobody knew many words and some were not sure of the middle part of the tune, but with a "la-la" and full lung-power it was triumphantly rendered from beginning to end. Of course everyone knew: "Aux armes, Citoyens! . . ." and "Marchons! Marchons! . . ."

And we gave it all we had.

After this diversion, with a profusion of "Merci Messieurs!" from Madame and family, who all crowded, beaming, into the doorway, more wine was passed round and the singing inevitably followed. "London's Burning" and other rounds; "Clementine", during which Mac grew soulful; and then Fred the Quartermaster's song. This was led by Fred and finally built itself up, verse by verse, into a complete melange of limb and body wagging—"one-finger—one-thumb—one-arm—two-arms—one-leg—two-legs—one nod-of-the-head—stand-up—sit-down—keep moving," it went, and we all threw ourselves about.

Then came another diversion, when Duncan's batman, Private Wheeler, who had helped to prepare the feast, appeared at the door with bleeding lip and dramatically announced in a trembling voice:

"It's Corporal Wallace, sir, he's just 'it me."

Corporal Wallace was a man of massive conscientiousness who brooded over "A" Company's transport lines. He was, in fact, Transport Corporal, and in his more carefree moments was prone to burst into a lifelike imitation of the Copshaw Special—a train that wandered about once a month through the remote part of Scotland whence he came. Private Wheeler, on the other hand, was strictly speaking a driver-batman, and Corporal Wallace not unreasonably conceived that Wheeler owed allegiance to him, Wallace, in equal part with his other and more domestic duties. Wheeler was one of his drivers. And he became incensed by a tendency on Private Wheeler's part simply to walk out on such things as sumps and carburettors—with rather untactful language—for his other duties whenever he so felt. Tonight, with the party on, it had been the last straw, and the blow had been struck.

Duncan rose from his place without a word and disappeared to judge between Private Wheeler and the wrath of the unseen Wallace. But he was back in a couple of minutes. He knew his men.

The singing continued unabated. There were interminable ditties—"Green Grow the Rushes-O", "Ten Green Bottles" and many others. Then Mac, normally the soberest of Scots but now well in his cups, announced: "I now take great pleasure in rendering you, to the memory of Colonel Ben, D.S.O., the 'Mountains of Mourne'."

And with the image in our minds of the figure with glass in one hand and monocle a-dangling, wreathed in the curling cigarette smoke of old Guest Nights back home, we supplied the chorus with fervour. . . .

THE WINTER

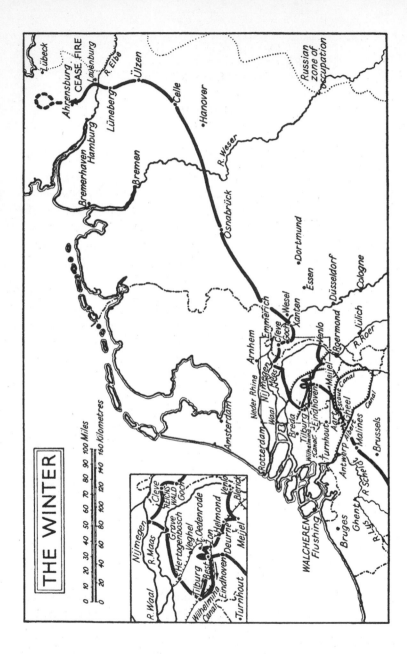

THE WINTER

0 10 20 30 40 50 60 70 80 90 100 Miles
0 20 40 60 80 100 120 140 160 Kilometres

Lübeck
Ahrensburg CEASE FIRE
Lauenburg
R. Elbe
Uelzen
Lüneburg
Celle
Bremerhaven
Hamburg
Hanover
Bremen
R. Weser
Osnabrück
Russian zone of occupation
Dortmund
Essen
Düsseldorf
Cologne
Emmerich
Wesel
Xanten
Cleve
Goch
Venlo
R. Jülich
Roermond
R. Roer
Arnhem
Neder Rhine
Nijmegen
Waal
Maas
Meijel
Aa
Escaut Canal
Wilhelmina Canal
Eindhoven
Tilburg
Breda
Turnhout
Gheel
Antwerp Albert Canal
Malines
Brussels
Rotterdam
Amsterdam
Ghent
Bruges
Flushing
WALCHEREN
R. Lys
R. Scheldt

Nijmegen
R. Waal
Cleve
R. Maas
REICHS WALD
Goch
Grave
's Hertogenbosch
Veghel
Oedenrode
Best
Tilburg
St.
Helmond
Venlo
Blerick
Eindhoven
Wilhelmina Canal
Deurne
Meijel
Turnhout

CHAPTER SIXTEEN

MAQUIS

DURING the halt over the Seine we were occupied by the mopping up of largely mythical pockets of Germans, in co-operation with the Maquis. Whatever enemy had been left behind invariably took to the forests, and the estimated strengths of these pockets would vary over anything up to a battalion or even more. The procedure was that the Maquis first suspected them, and came to us for aid. We then sallied out. With Maquis guides marching beside each platoon, we crashed through countless forests and got terribly hot. On the last day of August the entire Brigade toiled out and drew blank, and our weary Battalion returned to billets in the evening to discover that a body of Germans in hiding near by had been rounded up by the cooks in our absence. . . . So the upshot was that we never found a single German on any of these excursions, but ate an awful lot of blackberries.

However, prior to these more formal operations I had my own private war. This turned out to be rather fun.

For there came to our village the leader of the local Maquis, attended by his second-in-command. They sought Battalion Headquarters, and shortly I was sent for. Arriving at the comfortable farmhouse where B.H.Q. were installed, I found Giles the C.O. with the two Frenchmen. Giles indicated the Maquis leader: a virile looking man of about forty, carrying a gun and dressed in beret and shooting-jacket, who had visited England several times before the war, including my own home town, and who spoke good English. I was introduced, and he introduced me to his second-in-command. Giles then explained.

Before the advance the Maquis had buried a hoard of arms

and ammunition in a wood a few miles away, to hide them from the enemy. Now, in order to continue with the good work of rounding up Germans, they wanted to get at these again; but Germans had been seen in the same wood. So I was going to help them gain the wood and give protection if it still proved to be occupied. I was to have a rifle platoon from "A" Company, a carrier section from Support Company under command, and a wireless link to Battalion in case of trouble. A village two or three miles out was shown to me on the map, where I was to rendezvous. It was now about 10am, and the leader would be waiting for me at that village church at midday.

The two Frenchmen went their way in great spirits, Giles turned to other things, and I returned to "A" Company convinced I was going to certain suicide. From the map it was a big wood, and I foresaw unspecified numbers of very desperate Germans lurking in it.

My old 7 Platoon were selected to go with me, and there was one of the sharpest of tiffs with Duncan. Duncan had been very difficult of late. Highly strung at the best of times, he lived on his nerves here in France. He also possessed a most useful little map-case with all the right maps inserted and marked up. . . . Could I borrow the map-case for this Maquis business? No, I could not, and I should bloody well take the trouble to organize my own map-case. Well I never used a map-case in normal actions, but this was different—we were going out into the Blue. Duncan couldn't care less where we were going, and it was no reason to come plaguing him. Well, I didn't see why we should have to bloody well get killed for lack of a map-case he didn't need today and he would bloody well have it back in the evening. Well, it was his map-case and he happened to be commanding this Company, and I wasn't bloody well going to have it, and if we got killed it was my own bloody fault. And with this acrimonious beginning the carrier section turned up, and away we marched. Without the map-case.

It was a fine day. We set off into the fluid kind of no-man's land that France off the main routes of the armoured divisions had become, and the village of the rendezvous came into sight. We reached the church just before twelve and found the leader waiting. A large platoon of Maquis were drawn up in the street. There were some mutual salutations and a wonderful look came into the leader's face when he saw Sergeant MacEwan's men, and I was taken into a house next to the church where the curé evidently lived. He was small and elderly, and in appearance quite the dirtiest priest I had ever seen. For all his black cassock he fairly smacked of the soil and honest earthy labours. He bustled outside.

I was taken into a comfortable study. The leader with some pride passed a few remarks on the Maquis organization in the district, and drew from a carefully locked drawer a large map of the wood where we were going. Under the heel of the Occupation all had been organized with the finest craft. The map was spread over a large writing-bureau, and the leader, his second-in-command and I studied it. A loose plan was made. He impressed me, this Maquis leader; he was a natural soldier.

Emerging outside again, we found Jocks and the platoon of Maquis fraternizing busily, the old curé going round with a bucket and ladling out milk, and the village folk standing about and joining in the "entente". They were magnificent, these young Frenchmen. One looked into the fresh bronzed faces and saw the France that had not been conquered. Superbly fit and hardy, most of them were extremely young, and many were students. But they had forsaken all to join the Maquis, their uniform merely berets and armbands, with some sort of rifle and a few precious rounds of ammunition. And after the years of stealth, this was their hour. They came from many parts of France: some from Paris, one tall young fellow from the Jura Mountains, and only a few were local.

The leader and I quickly briefed our respective men and we all set off together. After a short march we came to the wood.

Then began what must have been one of the more extraordinary evolutions in the history of warfare.

The wood was approached by a wide, gently undulating cornfield shaven to stubble by the harvest. I despatched the three carriers of the carrier section to act as stops at vantage points covering the face and flanks of the wood, and so far so good. But it then appeared that the Frenchmen were going slap for it regardless of any use of cover at all. I suggested to the leader that we might each advance by our own route and meet there, and fortunately he agreed. The platoon of Maquis then surged forward in a great extended line with the leader out in front, and pressed forward at a sharp walk straight over every skyline all the way. If there had been one or two spandaus along the edge of the wood they would have leapt to engage them at the lift of the leader's little finger, and with the utmost valour would have been slaughtered.

Meanwhile, failing to see why we should suffer a similar fate I snaked with 7 Platoon on approximately the same course, using every conceivable fold in the ground but keeping an eye on them for most of the distance, and thus prudently convoying them. This meant quite a lot of zig-zagging, took us five or ten minutes longer to get there, would have assuredly earned us full marks on any battle-school exercise in fieldcraft, and seemed vaguely ridiculous. But if the wood had been defended, most of us would have had a chance of getting there. . . . However, it was not defended. There was nobody in it. So everyone got there.

There was nothing much left to do. We crept through the trees and the Maquis found their spot, and while they dug for the weapons and ammunition we took up positions around them. Eventually, after the most amiable au revoirs, we returned into the fold of Ben's Battalion and I reported on it all to Giles.

Late that night members of the same party of Maquis shepherded quite a haul of German prisoners into Battalion Headquarters. These had been captured by means of the same weapons we had helped them to retrieve, and the leader sent us a message of thanks.

On next seeing Giles he told me he had repeated to the leader that I had thought him a fine soldier, and that the leader had shown much pleasure.

The "entente" flourished.

CHAPTER SEVENTEEN

THE GREAT SWAN SONG

WITHIN a week, with "Bonne Chance" in our ears from the family in our villa, we were off. . . . It is an old story now; but it remains one of the moments of a lifetime.

We swept northwards. All the way a dark shadow receded before us, and the fleeting phantom of the Occupation became almost tangible. We followed a trail of hate the enemy had left behind them—whether France, Belgium or up in the Netherlands, it was always the same—exceeding anything we had imagined.

Most of the way we were carried by the R.A.S.C., by troop-carrying companies, supply companies, petrol companies, by anything with wheels that could be thrown together. Although in the general wake of the armoured spearheads, we went mainly off the beaten track, up roads where no previous British troops had passed. We motored preceded by our armoured reconnaissance units, ready to debus, deploy and fight a battle the instant we bumped anything. We drove through few towns at first, and through mile upon mile of flat, empty wastes of countryside. And when we were not motoring we were marching. Debussing to allow the lorries to go back for more infantry, and marching to the next embussing point for transport again. The story was told of a British and a German convoy driving together for miles by night, intermixed, each in the belief that the other was of the same nationality. Strange captured enemy vehicles made mysterious appearances among our columns, under the newly stencilled colours of our heraldry. And lost German soldiers sometimes broke into the roadway with their hands up.

We were all curious to see the battlefields of the first war, but we swished across all four years of them in two days, and saw next to nothing. The Somme we crossed somewhere west of Amiens. The first town of note we went through was St Pol. We crossed the Calais-Arras highway, and bending north-east we skirted close to Béthune and La Bassée, heading for Lille and the frontier, where enemy rearguards were reported. And at a halt near La Bassée we saw the only 1914-18 war cemetery of our journey, It was a small British one by the roadside where "A" Company's lorries had stopped, and many of the Company jumped out and wandered bareheaded among the graves, carrying their steel helmets in their hands. A number of the graves were found to be of men of our own Regiment; and here, for just the ten minutes of a roadside halt, the streams of past and present crossed. The headstones had green moss growing up from their bases, like teeth untended, and the grass was unkempt, but nothing had been defaced.

Further northwards towns and villages became more frequent, and as we approached the dense industrial region around Lille and the frontier the acclaims of the population rose to an endless shout. Our progress took the appearance of a royal procession. It was fantastic. For mile after mile as we drove along, the people of every town, village and wayside hamlet seemed to be out *en masse* to cheer us. Our lorries were pelted with flowers, plums, pears, tomatoes, bottles of beer, biscuits, wine and even plain bread. Everything they could offer us was handed up over our running-boards. At every momentary stop trays of drinks and fruit were at our elbows. All the flags were out. Frequently the convoy was reduced to a crawl as the lorries forged carefully through lanes of people cheering themselves hoarse and clambering up to shake our hands. Pathetic, proud old men, obviously old soldiers, stood at the salute as we came by. Some of the very old must have remembered 1870. Others were Maquis with their rifles and armbands. Women and children were there in thousands. Even in villages battered by the R.A.F. the reception was the same. Miles of smiles and laughter, and tears. Everywhere the shouts of "Nos amis!". . . "Vive les Anglais!". . . The accordions playing "Tipperary". . . . And the voice in broken English from some Frenchman clinging to the running-board to shake you by the hand: "We are very pleased to see you." It was so spontaneous, and before each village we began to half-dread the welcome we knew would be unloosed at us. A lump rose to the throat and the eyes misted. The last straw was at a hamlet where four solitary figures stood with rifles at the "Present", motionless, as lorry after lorry of our troops rumbled past: they were the local group of Maquis, in front of a 1914-18 war memorial. While at a railway crossing near Lille a mob of people were dragging the dead body of a German soldier through the dust, and gesticulating and shouting to draw our attention, and dancing upon it for joy.

At the French frontier town of Halluin multitudes packed the main street and again the vehicles had to nose their way along at a crawl. The German rearguards had pulled out that same morning after a battle with the Maquis. The convoy halted—and we were engulfed. We were supposed to be crossing into Belgium by the Menin Gate, but the bridge over the River Lys had been blown and the reconnaissance units were probing for another crossing-place, with enemy rearguards on the far bank. Meanwhile the entire population of Halluin must have been surrounding us. They swarmed over the lorries. Girls with tricolour bows in their hair besieged us for kisses. Autographs were demanded from us. There was a howl, and out of a side street came a mob chasing a woman with a shaven head who had collaborated. A man repeatedly thrust his daughter into my arms. I was bade kiss three small schoolgirls, kiss a young woman and her baby, kiss two maidens who gave me their addresses and took mine—and I was cornered: I had been brought up in the straitjacket of an English public school, and "Don't be shy!" smote my ears in a voice exactly like that

138

of Corporal Wallace, mighty busy in the Company carrier next to me. . . . It was a riot. . . . But at last we moved on again. Then debussed and deployed to attack. Another bridge had been found, about three miles up the river. The Germans had tried to blow it, but the Belgian Resistance had kept it open for us: so over we went, and the Germans had gone. It was late evening, 6th September. Abruptly, the blue, white and red tricolour of France had been replaced everywhere by the black, yellow and red. We were in Belgium. . . . We entered the town of Wevelghem across the Lys bridge.

Nowhere were we treated with more kindness and more wonderfully welcomed by the civil population than in Belgium. The first night we spent in Wevelghem as part of a bridgehead over the Lys, but it was hard to get any operational duties done. Officers were regaled with invitations out to supper, breakfast invitations followed with the morning, and every family kept open house. The soldier had only to desire a wash and shave and he was instantly surrounded by every hospitality, and led away. For "elevenses" a family trooped without warning into the air-raid shelter occupied by "A" Company Headquarters bearing a large urn of coffee, tea, home-made cake, gingerbread, milk, butter and sugar. Pre-war cigars were dug from hiding-places—"for the day when you would come." Then we pushed on again and the royal procession continued, with banners proclaiming "Welcome: Our Liberators" in every place. We marched, heading for Ghent. Soon we had a line facing north-westwards along the Lys, which flows through Ghent. Elsewhere the Division mopped up the area eastwards between Ghent-Oudenarde-Courtrai. But enemy resistance had crumbled again and from high O.P.s in Courtrai their columns were seen toiling northwards. A company of the "Fusiliers" occupied a village astride one of the escape routes. "After killing or capturing all the Germans there," relates the Lowland Brigade account, "the company had an amusing night ambushing enemy convoys, which unsuspectingly kept driving into the place."

Meanwhile "A" Company had reached another village. This lay by the Lys, off the main road Wevelghem-Ghent. Unhappily a few days earlier a British armoured column had passed through, travelling northwards, so the populace had hung out the flags. But the next event was a retreating German column, travelling in the same direction. The enemy tore all the flags down again and proceeded to beat the place up. Many houses were shattered by the explosion when they blew the bridge. Then we arrived. The village turned out. "We have waited for you for four years," they cried.

Duncan, Colin and I were installed in a charming, well-appointed house. Here there was another Madame, short, very plump, very Belgian, and dressed in black. Two months earlier her younger son, aged nineteen, had killed a couple of Germans in helping an R.A.F. pilot to escape. The enemy had caught him and put him against a wall, and shot him. Her elder son was missing in the Resistance—the "White Guard". Her daughter-in-law had been carried off to Germany. Many of the people were dressed in mourning for such things. . . . We had to organize operational positions. "The Germans take everything, but you ask," said the plump little Madame in black. . . . There was also a Monsieur, grey-headed, who hovered in the background unable to speak English, and obviously a breadwinner of ability. Also an extremely pretty young daughter of about fourteen. She wanted my glengarry as a souvenir, so I gave her a cap-badge. Out in the paddock there was a foal called "Eden".

We were two nights there, and were entertained with marvellous kindness. The house was ours. Champagne, wine, cigars—even a radio—were dug up from the garden where they had been hidden from the enemy. Colin and I accepted a dinner invitation from the Mayor, but heard from Duncan that this was causing distress to our Madame in black. Apparently the Mayor was by no means untainted by collaborationism and had been instrumental in getting Madame's younger son caught. Here in Belgium they were shooting the collaborators. They were smashing their houses and painting swastikas over them. We sent a note to the Mayor saying we were "occupé" and unable to dine.

The last night the young daughter wished to bestow kisses upon us. We were lined up in the drawing-room in order of seniority, Duncan, myself and Colin, and received a whacking kiss a-piece: and it seemed to me we were returning the compliment rather. . . . Next morning we moved off. Madame said I was like her son. "After ze war," she said, "you come back and stay here with your girl many days." Everyone trooped out to see us off. Madame placed a large bouquet of flowers and a Belgian flag on the bonnet of Duncan's truck at the head of the column. "Where do you go now?" they asked. "A Berlin!" cried Duncan. And in front of all "A" Company Madame gave me two plump kisses, one on each cheek, and we drove out. With exceeding resolve on the further prosecution of this war we waved farewell to our Madame in black. "A Berlin" it would be.

We went into a concentration area at Zemst, near Malines. As we drove through Zemst the ancient carillon rang out Scottish tunes in our honour. Brussels had just been liberated and that evening some liberty trucks were run there. There was another row with Duncan. I thought we were all going to Brussels. My glengarry was out, my shoes were on my feet. But no. I was staying behind on duty in the Company. And with some other officers, packed in a jeep, Duncan went.

We were here another day, then off again: there were a lot of Germans holding the Albert Canal to the north. We reached Gheel.

Gheel. . . . Some names seemed to embody the fate they held for us. Gheel resounded across our path like the blare of a gong, and brought to an end our great swan song. We found

141

grim humour in the fact that we had stopped being liberators. We had to fight a war again, and fought a battle that stood among the fiercest of our campaign. For at Gheel the glare of Normandy was briefly rekindled.

Gheel was a small town with a spire and a convent midway among the three or four miles that separated the Albert and Escaut canals. We went into a shattering assembly area in the middle of a regimental gun-position of 25-pounders, and at dusk moved across a Bailey bridge over the Albert Canal, and through a bridgehead formed by the Tyne and Tees Division. We spent an alerted, pitch-black night, with shelling from both sides, among the fields and farmhouses in front of the black spire of Gheel. Strewn about "A" Company's area were the unpleasant remains of a Northumbrian platoon who had been surprised by an enemy attack that morning and wiped out.

Next day it appeared that the enemy had melted back to the Escaut. We stole through Gheel town, and everywhere passed abandoned German dug-outs and command posts littered with rubbish and empty champagne bottles. The spire had been an enemy O.P. and was shot through. We came out the other side of the town into positions a mile or so ahead, with the Recce Regiment feeling up to the line of the Escaut. It started to rain. Another pitch-black night descended.

Late in the night "A" Company were ordered to rush a footbridge over the Escaut, believed still to be standing but which had not been reconnoitred. This was on the Brigade Commander's instructions, and was a mournful business.

CHAPTER EIGHTEEN

THE PASSING OF DUNCAN

"HOW is he, sir?"

It was twelve hours later. I was in the back of the C.O.'s jeep. Giles was wearing his harassed expression. He turned round sharply in his seat beside the driver.

"Oh, didn't you know?—he's dead."

"Dead?" I said.

My mind went back to England, to the same Giles telling me about the smash of Victor Sylvest in the same sort of way. Wearily I heard him explaining. . . . "got him back to the dressing station . . . terribly badly hurt, of course . . . died early this morning . . . dreadful pity. . . ."

Loneliness filled me. Duncan, through the very force of that unique personality, had surely been invincible. And the confident, hale and hearty voice from the stretcher the night before rang again in my ears:

"Bash on, Woolbags. Kill lots of bloody Boches!"

So had he handed over "A" Company to me. He would come striding back as awkward as ever in a couple of weeks, I had been thinking, half wishfully, just as he had done before in Normandy.

But Duncan would not come back this time; nor had the Escaut been crossed. And whatever might next befall "A" Company, it was up to me now. . . . Withdrawing from the enemy and the floodwater they had unloosed. Giles breezing up in the morning to see how the Company were. Giles driving me back towards Gheel to show me the new line. Giles being harassed, but sympathetic so far as one had ever seen him, and allotting the Company an area at B.H.Q. where we would stay in reserve for a while. And of the five company officers last New Year's Eve, only myself left. Because Duncan was dead.

Even his passing had been in keeping with the manner in which he had lived.

He was a man you could only come across once in a lifetime. One of his ancestors, kinsman of the Conqueror, had held high office in the host at Senlac. And in the due course of the lineage, which took root in Scotland and was turbulent, he was born, in a baronial hall in the Highlands. Weaned at Eton, he went into the Regular Army by way of a wine business and the supplementary reserve, shortly before the outbreak of war.

But these were the things one gleaned. He never talked of them. I knew next to nothing of his private life.

The sergeant-major, who knew him at Dunkirk, said he was always the same. He was large. Noisy. Hectic. Disturbing. His boots were large. He had double soles on them. His legs covered a large ground surface. He was a mass of complexities and contradictions. He was like some great striding, extrovert Hamlet: one cannot interpret all his parts. His whole nature was a flourish.

In appearance he was indeed like a great Viking. He was tall—not an exaggerated height, but considerably over six feet, with his very long legs; and very blond. He carried himself splendidly, although he did not look noticeably athletic. But it was his presence that was striking. The hair was worn long and brushed back above the ears, and a lock occasionally wandered across the side of his forehead. He scorned anything but the most perfunctory concessions around the nape of the neck to King's Regulations, and was apt to cultivate small tufts on the cheekbones. The face was dominated by a fair, sweeping moustache that covered the whole of a high upper lip and largely hid the mouth: a not very full mouth, rather petulant, and surprisingly sensitive. The chin, of good length, receded

144

slightly. One was never quite sure if it was a weak chin. The nose was finely cast, with a firm, well-shaped bridge to it; the forehead clear, definite, a shade narrow. The eyes were pale blue, and out of sheer innate shyness they never held the gaze of the person he was talking to—unless angry, when they grew curiously baleful and one almost saw them glow. In all, an effective, though not a conventionally strong face. It could betray his intensely highly strung nature, and it showed a degree of almost fierce obstinacy. But it had something more: it was an indefinably aristocratic face. It was born for a beard—this effect would have been startling. Then put the man in trunk-hose, doublet and ruff, fasten sword and buckle to him, throw a sable cloak over his shoulders, and you would see before you the living incarnation of an Elizabethan nobleman; or better, some courtier to one of the last Stuart kings. It was a shame he had to wear battle-dress.

You knew when he was talking. He had a peculiarly throaty voice. An obstinate voice. A sophisticated voice; but too alive, too definite, for a drawl. Assertive and truculent by turn. You could tell when he was going to be awkward by the voice. It was a boisterous voice: "Where's that bloody colour-sergeant?" it demanded once upon a time in Company office—"he's never here when I want him and always here when I don't want him." And the worried face of a little man we called Three Bags Full Sir, who was then colour-sergeant, promptly appeared round the partition with its habitual yessir-nossir-pleassir. And nobody but Duncan uttered things like that, and nobody but Duncan could have carried them off with such aplomb. But then nobody else commanded a company like a feudal overlord, a benevolent despot, and got away with it.

Then add a rollicking, cavalierish style at all times. A really penetrating wit. A great laugh that inhaled the air with staccato, rasping honks of mirth. A capacity for wilfulness to the point of being unpleasant. The heavy tread of his great boots. The extraordinary aura of restlessness, agitation and movement

145

that attended his person. The faint, quaint illusion that he was miscast for the twentieth century; yet see him as someone so completely of the times in which he lived. The heckling, bantering, jostling address; yet see someone genuinely very funny—but not a funny man. And perhaps you can see some reflection of the image of Duncan. See a dominating personality, wherever he went among his contemporaries; but see him as someone who, when the last count is taken, was somehow not domineering. He was too shy, his sensibility too strong, but you would have to know him for some time to see this. . . . See him as a great overgrown schoolboy, but with a power of perception and a *savoir faire* far beyond his years. For if you could really see him you would be surprised that he was only twenty-seven when he was killed.

He was a man with a tremendous appetite for life. In wartime soldiering he was in his element. He had to have drama. The man himself was dramatic, and war was dramatic. The most prosaic situation he could infuse with an element of drama, and it was his gift that he could fill subordinates with something of his own enthusiasm by giving the impression of assuming that they already had that enthusiasm. When issuing orders he appeared to be taking them into some entirely new, exciting and important confidence: they could not but respond to such drama.

He was a leader. "A" Company were his personal property for altogether three years: and in "A" Company his name was legend. With an especial flair for administration, he revelled in his rule, and delivered firm and undisputed justice from Company office, like a Solomon. Power was meat and drink to him, which was why he found it so difficult during the interlude of Gavin. His remarks could set a whole parade laughing; he treated the Jocks with an easy, humorous intimacy, and they knew he was more than their match. He was one of those not altogether common officers who was more proficient than his men in every department of their activities. He inspired smouldering resentments and abiding loyalties. He was a royal man.

To what extent he was liked would elude you. He seemed to take a perverse pleasure in riling, and had the reputation throughout the Battalion of being "bloody-minded". And his name was legend throughout the Battalion, for that matter. Autocratic and high-handed, his sense of duty inexorable and his attention to detail exhaustive, and exacting in the extreme to work for, you could indeed hate him one moment but do anything for him the next; while there was no gainsaying his efficiency. The man was a Big Picture in himself.

To his superiors he could be as awkward as a mule. It was hopeless to argue with him: on the rare occasions when he could not have his own way he simply grew truculent and aggressive. His brother officers would say that he could bluff his way through anything, but it was impossible to keep up any sustained dislike of him when at a moment's notice he could turn into a one-man pantomime. It was his wit that redeemed him. He broke through all defences.

He was a voracious pipe-smoker, incessantly blowing out clouds of tobacco and coughing, and using none but delicate little Dunhills. A cigarette he never touched. His toilet was fastidious. His nerves were fantastic. He could scarcely pass a cup of tea in one hand without upsetting it; when he poured sugar into his cup there was a flurry like a minor snowstorm. He ate like a horse, and had a huge capacity for drink. At parties he would be seen, dissipated, with the lock of hair nearly in his eyes, proclaiming with relish to all and sundry that he was "roué!—roué!" He never danced. Women never entered into his order of things. But once he did remark, and it was typical of the bizarre in the man, that if ever he married he would have the Grand March from "Aïda" played at the wedding; and I suppose to the end of my days the Grand March will bring to my mind Duncan. There is a lot of Duncan in it.

As for religion, he appeared to have none. But then he was

147

shy. How much of all the bluster was his defence took hold of you the longer you knew him, and remained a mystery. Sometimes he revealed a little more of himself. Compassion was not a part of him, but understanding was there and occasionally looked at you, or showed itself through leaving you alone. Some unexpected comment made in a quiet moment showed a true feeling for music. He could see beauty in things. He never made personal remarks about people, even in the wildest banter, as if afraid of retaliation. "An officer with an inferiority complex is finished," he told me once, and it seemed that he harboured some strain of bitterness or old complex himself to which he never owned: that his inner self he could not expose too far, for fear of its being hurt.

"You," said Giles the C.O. to me, "were well brought up—you had Duncan for your upbringing.". . . While soldiers who had known him would exclaim reminiscently, with chuckles and a touch of awe: "What a man!"

By the time we emerged from the battles in Normandy I think something in him had changed. The voice, the honks of mirth, the habits—the flourish that he made—were still there, but much of the rollicking bluster of old had died. He had grown older, or rather had aged. His temperament, ever difficult, often became impossible, yet in certain moments he had a new poise that had its dignity. And he quietly attended the Padre's services in rest areas, large and still obstinate, somewhere at the back.

In battle all his powers of drive and command were mobilized: first at himself, and then to the leadership of his Company against the enemy. Several times I saw when the hands were unsteadier than ever, but the rest of the Company never saw it, and his name remained legend. At times he seemed ruthless. Before an attack in Normandy he told his platoon commanders it did not matter if they were killed, so long as their platoons reached the objectives. I think the firmer he had to be with himself the harsher he had to be with others, and

148

this resulted in excitability and temper in a crisis.

One afternoon at Estry I was beside him in his trench when we were mortared. We could hear the thumps of the bombs leaving the distant barrels. "Listen," he breathed, "they're mortaring us!" He gripped my arm. He was afraid.

The end came at the footbridge on the Escaut Canal.

At 10.30 that night he was suddenly called away from our farmhouse to Battalion Headquarters. He was back before long, forcedly calm, and I knew it was bad. The "O" Group were called at once. By the light of his torch on the map he gave a usual forceful briefing. The Brigade Commander wanted the bridge captured intact. At midnight "A" Company were to rush it. Colin's platoon would make the capture. We would hold a small bridgehead the other side, and at four o'clock in the morning the rest of the Battalion were to pass through. Anti-tank guns towed by jeeps, for lightness and silence, were moving with the Company in case the bridge would stand them. Enemy strength and positions were unknown, but it was thought there were none this side of the canal. We were to move off straight away.

When the others had gone, he turned to me with a kind of tired resignation:

"Well, what do you make of this one?" He was shaken. It was the only occasion he had sought my opinion.

"I expect they've pulled back," I said. They had pulled back from the Albert Canal. "It may be all right," I said. But he was sure they were on the Escaut. Why should they leave a crossing-place wide open?

"If they are, I've got to judge when we get there whether it's a feasible operation," he said. "If they're in strength I've got to sit tight and hold our bank."

We marched the odd thousand yards down to the bridge. The road was straight. The Company in single file by platoons, in the night. Myself at the rear of the column with main Company Headquarters. A short way behind nosed the jeeps with their anti-tank guns. Away at the head of the column was Duncan, with his decision, and Gordon of the anti-tanks who marched with him to help him weigh up the situation when we got there. The night was inky, and it was raining steadily.

The last few hundred yards the road dipped through woods to the canal bank. It was midnight, with a solid blackness through the woods. No sound but the stealthy crunching of our boots, the occasional slight rattle of a rifle butt banging against a tree trunk, and the eerie patter of the rain on the leaves. There was a halt.

The enemy were waiting for us. Four "Eighty-eights" had been sited along the far bank to cover the bridge, together with a number of multiple-mounted anti-aircraft "flak" guns, that were fired along the ground with devastating effect. In an instant the woods became an echoing inferno. Sniping seemed to break out from all directions and the few yards of flat ground between the edge of the trees and the water were alive with fire. And there was no bridge. The road bridge had been blown and there was only a pair of lock gates, along which ran a catwalk. Only Colin and the first section of 8 Platoon got across. Two were killed and the rest taken prisoner, except for Colin himself: saved by the sound of the rain on the water, he later managed to crawl back to our side again. The German trenches were twenty yards from the water's edge, in the woods opposite.

A few moments after the din broke out my name was called urgently down the line of men, from voice to voice, and the name of Duncan. He was hit. Frantically I blundered forward through the blackness, through the commotion, to the top of the Company. I ran into Gordon of the anti-tanks. He shouted in my ear: "You're to hold this bank; you're to line this dyke." There was a dyke parallel to the canal along the edge of the wood; and he disappeared into the night to his guns. And Duncan's voice was calling me. "Here I am," I answered.

He was on the ground, on a stretcher, a blanket over him. I ran to him. He saw me, and then the boisterous tones of old rang out above the firing:

"Bash on, Woolbags. Kill lots of bloody Boches!"

Suddenly I could have wept for him. We had spoken the same language. For a moment I dropped on one knee beside the stretcher. I felt an arm, and patted it. "Good luck," I said. He made no reply. It was too dark to see his face beyond a blur. I doubled off to take his place, and they carried him away. When he had gone forward to make his decision, one of the "flak" guns had got him. His arms and legs were broken. Afterwards one of the stretcher-bearers who ran to him was muttering that he had cried out, "Shoot me, Gordon. . . ."

The rest of the night dragged out. Our wireless had been hit and we were out of touch with Battalion. We lined the dyke up to our waists in water. The rain pelted. Gradually the din petered out into a black wet silence with the constant patter of rain. Then the water-level in the dyke began to rise. The enemy had operated the sluice gates somewhere and were flooding us. I collected the platoon commanders, all sergeants. We groped a short way back into the black wood and I gave them fresh positions like blind man's buff. The Company withdrew to them, then Colin turned up from the other side, offering to go back and search for his lost men; but it was no use.

At daylight we were shelled again. Later I crept forward with binoculars to the edge of the trees and saw two Germans, also with binoculars, peering through the undergrowth on the other side.

The floods were now seeping steadily through the woods and our trenches were getting swamped. Giles breezed up, and we pulled back.

And Duncan was dead.

"Finis" was ironically written to the passing of Duncan the following night.

Each Company owned two carriers. Long ago it had been decreed by Colonel Ben that these were to be named after

151

localities in the regimental territorial district: the name of each carrier being neatly stencilled upon it, and beginning with the designation letter of the Company to which it belonged, for easier recognition. Throughout the Battalion it was so—except for Duncan's carriers. Typically these were christened "Storm" and "Stormrie", after the baronial fief and the baronial hall respectively, which hardly began with an "A" and were not in the regimental district either. But nobody had the energy to make him alter them.

The day we pulled back from the floods the "Royals" gained a bridgehead at a village called Aart, a mile or two up the canal. By evening a pontoon raft was functioning and the whole Brigade were over, to be consistently shelled and counter-attacked by enemy parachute troops. During the night a lurid firework display broke out from behind "A" Company's trenches, with blown-up ammunition erupting and causing weird fires that flickered away through the dark hours until dawn. It was Storm and Stormrie that had both received direct hits from heavy shells.

CHAPTER NINETEEN

TWO'S COMPANY

WHILE we were in the bridgehead at Aart—we called it by the general name of the Gheel bridgehead—the airborne armada for the descent on the Netherlands passed over our heads; but down below at Aart on the Escaut Canal we had a private "Arnhem".

We were puzzled as to what was being achieved by the severe fighting here, and by the vehemence of the enemy's reaction. The idea had been to force a way of advance into Holland for the Second Army. The Brigade fought for three days and four nights, lost over five hundred men, and in the meantime the main thrust of the Army developed elsewhere. Finally the bridgehead was abandoned altogether.

However, we undoubtedly slew many enemy, and afterwards received the thanks of the commander of the corps leading the drive up Holland. For there proved to be considerable numbers of Germans at large in northern Belgium and the Netherlands and at least we had drawn some of them away from the troops battling up the corridor to Arnhem. Later it was learnt that the German First Parachute Army, holding this area, had received categorical orders to deny the crossing of the Escaut to 15th Scottish Division. Selected troops were reorganized with SS officers and N.C.O.s, and sent to Aart.

Aart was a small village on the north bank of the canal. It possessed a church, a village school and a small factory. "A" Company, on crossing into the bridgehead, were superimposed over the positions of a tattered company of the "Royals", whose headquarters had been overrun and all their officers captured. One of their platoons had been overpowered in hand-to-hand fighting around a farm cottage, and their battalion, which had been first across and had suffered heavily, were later withdrawn. Thereafter our Battalion and the "Fusiliers" alone held the village. The bridgehead now measured some five hundred yards across and about six hundred yards in depth, and there it remained.

A few miles to the north was the site of the pre-war Belgian Army artillery school at Bourg Leopold, with the artillery practice ranges at Turnhout. These the Germans had utilized, and from there directed an unceasing stream of expert and accurate gunfire at us. The main road from Turnhout down to Gheel ran straight as a die through Aart, and they also used to shoot along it with high-velocity support guns. In the end it was impossible to get a Bailey bridge built, so that little heavy equipment could be passed over the canal. The Sappers managed to maintain the pontoon raft, and anti-tank guns and carriers were handled over, otherwise only foot soldiers could be moved into the cramped bridgehead—over the raft.

We lived like moles, clinging to our slit-trenches in the sandy soil, and beat off thirteen counter-attacks, several of which came in battalion strength supported by tanks. Our gunner O.P.s were shot out of the church spire and shot off the factory roof—or at least they should have been, only they just stayed on. Our perimeter was ringed with defensive fire-tasks laid from the gun areas around Gheel town, and it was quite a sensation when in answer to your own voice a complete field regiment came crashing down on to some danger zone ahead of the Company front. But soon there was an ammunition shortage, because everything was going into the effort to link-up with the airborne forces, and the shells were rationed.

In spite of everything a number of prisoners were taken, many of whom came from the Hermann Goering Regiment. Their commanders had told them they were fighting "crack Scottish infantry". We agreed, although it was gratifying to hear it from the other side.

154

At the same time the floodwater in the canal, unleashed by the enemy, steadily rose. Parts of the surrounding countryside were already several feet under water and it was a question of some urgency as to when we should have to swim for it. But at Aart the water eventually halted two feet from the top of the bank.

And here, in "A" Company, was the compact little entity of Company Headquarters in this sandy soil, with the battered houses along the village street about a hundred yards at our backs. Everyone was sharing a slit-trench with someone else, as usual, except me, by some chance. Which was not so good. For the world consisted of heads. Heads of sentries, heads of relief sentries, lurking heads, heads chewing bars of chocolate, and expressionless, heads slightly oscillating as rifles were cleaned, heads that sometimes blew their noses on dirty handkerchiefs, heads that looked at one another across the tops of their trenches throughout the daylight hours. Hour after hour. Those heads of "A" Company. Heads under steel helmets with unshaven faces, with all the imponderable fortitude of the British soldier upon them, heads that all disappeared below the ground as if pulled by the same string whenever another load of shells came down—but nobody else in my trench. Nobody to share a laboured joke, no solid body drawing at a cigarette in the corner opposite. Even my signallers a universe away, the other side of three or four feet of this earth.

I used to wonder what all the other heads were doing at the moment. Inanely I tried to visualize them, but each trench was a world of its own, with infinite distance separating it from its neighbour; each a separate world, sheltering its human life, on its own particular brink of eternity. I never remembered these imaginings in Normandy, and alone in the trench I grasped the floor of it and twisted the sand in my hands: and down came more sand, tumbling down the sides as the trench shuddered from near misses. And because there was nobody there, there was nobody to overhear, I spoke aloud. The Lord's Prayer, the Creed, the General Confession—they were my repertoire, and I went through the lot. Sometimes, on the spur of the moment, I composed my own. When I reached the end, if the shelling still continued, I started over again at the beginning. When at last there came a stunning silence all the heads bobbed up again, and looked round to see if all the other heads were the same, and I was once more the Company Commander. If someone was hit, the stretcher-bearers would be already doubling out to his cries, and when the next dose came over the string was pulled and down we all ducked again.

Then, in the middle of an afternoon, a youthful member of the Sniper Section took shelter with me. We had been troubled by hostile snipers working through the scrubland in front of our positions and causing us casualties. The plan was to set a pair of our own snipers to hunt them, with instructions to report to me before starting out. So he arrived, in advance of his mate, and waited for him in my trench.

We exchanged remarks: trivialities about home, the next relief, about things forgotten within the hour. He offered me a cigarette and fell to cleaning his rifle and telescopic sights, a tuft of hair protruding under the lining of his helmet. I had not come across him in the Battalion before, and he talked quietly as he worked at his rifle, with a smile now and then, not particularly tense about what he must do. Low over the ground broke the occasional whip-crack of a German sniper's bullet. A few salvoes hissed overhead to splatter among the houses or smite the ferry site. Sagged about and scattered down the village street the lone bodies of German paratroopers slowly rotted, sacrificed and mutilated through hopeless acts of bravado; you stepped over them every time you went back to the command post at the canal. One of them had headed a rush down the street at the "Royals", waving a white flag and shouting "Tommy—surrender!" He had been shot down and there he lay, partially naked, a sneer still fixed on his blue lips.

156

Putting aside his rifle, my companion produced a crumpled pad of notepaper from his haversack and wrote a short letter home. Before long his mate arrived on the scene: this was evidently the Number One of the pair, a much older and rather wild looking individual. The other collected his equipment together and climbed out of my trench. He turned to leave the letter he had written in my care, to go back with the next mail, and without more ado they set off together. I watched them make their way through a small orchard held by 7 Platoon and cautiously disappear into the scrub beyond.

Towards evening the older man reappeared in a dreadful state, alone. The sergeant-major took charge of him and pieced together his story from a string of savage oaths and imprecations. I listened in.

"Of course I got him—I got him the next minute," he fiercely asserted; and the sergeant-major despatched him back to B.H.Q.

I turned away.

CHAPTER TWENTY

THE DAY'S WORK

COUNTER-ATTACKS at Aart happened with regularity around 8 o'clock in the mornings and at dusk. And often during the dark hours we could hear enemy transport moving down from Turnhout, the distant plopping of a motorbike, or the clinking of tanks and other tracked vehicles prowling about.

One morning a voice shouted to me from a nearby bren team: "Sir!—Sir!—are those Jerries?" I jumped to my parapet with the binoculars, and out to our flank two or three long waves of infantrymen were advancing upon "D" Company's positions on our right. Wearing capes like our groundsheets and carrying their rifles at the trail like we did, they were coming in so obviously that one certainly wondered for a moment if the were not our own troops. But they were Germans all right. The nearest were barely a couple of hundred yards from us. "They're enemy—fire!" I yelled—"fire!" and hurriedly blew the stand-to on my whistle: the first wave was almost abreast of us in perfect enfilade. At the same moment firing broke out from further along and someone brought mortars down, and they all dropped to the ground, hidden. Then the guns opened up, and what became of them was unclear.

We were on the west side of the perimeter. Another morning an attack came in at "B" Company in the north-east sector, and the enemy succeeded in reoccupying that part of the village. "C" Company down by the canal on the west side, on our left, were speedily ordered across to halt the penetration at the point of their bayonets. The situation was stabilized. It was then decided to relieve them by a second company which was to clear the enemy out altogether. For this further task "A" Company were selected, and I received a wireless call from the command post.

The command post was in the last house at the bottom of the village street, next to the canal, in a very deep cellar. And here, for three days and four nights, at the hub of our wireless network, dwelt Giles the C.O. There could hardly have been a more tenacious Briton in Aart. Main B.H.Q. was the far side of the canal, and he was attended only by Hugh the I.O. Sundry signallers, runners and medical orderlies were squeezed about the place and up the stairs, and down they all stumbled whenever a renewed stonking fell outside. To add to the scrum the "Fusiliers", holding the east side of the village, were sharing the same command post.

I was given my instructions: it would be a street and house clearing operation, to be carried out with two platoons, with my third platoon left behind to hold our normal area. It was now midday, and 1.30pm was fixed for our zero hour.

I returned to the Company, 7 and 9 Platoons were warned to stand by, and with the platoon sergeants I snatched a quick reconnaissance. Our objective consisted of a single street that led eastwards into open country from a crossroads on that side of the village, and the task was to clear to the end of the houses. The view up the road was limited by a bend at a white house, which was occupied by the forward platoon of our own troops.

At 1.30 we were forming up to move off, behind the Company positions. Then a rude distraction. Planes swooped overhead, skimming feet above the house-tops. There was a deafening crackle of cannon fire and everyone leapt into the ditch. Cannon shells ripped into some of the houses: but they were our own R.A.F. Typhoons, and there was a great swishing and vast thuds. The ground shook as their rockets smote enemy positions only a few hundred yards away. Quantities of yellow smoke, denoting the positions of our own troops to the R.A.F., billowed upwards from the Company trenches, where the sergeant-major was hopping about igniting canisters. The whirlwind performance was as quickly over, and we picked ourselves up and set off.

We moved a short way up the village street and took a turning to the right by the scarred church. The spire was riddled with shell holes and the roof gaped. We moved down the turning a short distance until we came to the crossroads. It was a large crossroads where a bypass went down to the canal. Not a living soul stirred. Every house was a ruin and every open plot of ground churned by craters. It was like a place of the dead. Straight opposite was the start of the street we were to clear. As we approached the crossroads one or two voices called out from somewhere, piercing an uneasy stillness: "You'd better run across the road." A few slits in the earth that had wondrously survived the cratering were noticeable at the roadside, with tired looking men of "B" Company looking up at us from them.

There was no need for their advice. In section groups we sprinted for it, but the German O.P.s must have been watching. Even while we ran a rapid succession of thumps battered out from high-velocity guns in the near distance. For an awful instant the air was filled with a fast-coming whistle, then scores of shells slammed into the crossroads with tremendous speed and accuracy. The enemy gunners were now busy. The thumps, whistling and crashes of exploding shells were simultaneous, and a sustained concentration turned the area into a hell.

On the left of the street that we were to attack was the village school, and on the right an orchard wall; then a few houses on either side, and further up on the right the white house at the bend. There had to be a momentary halt for the platoons to collect again, and the shelling rained on us. 7 Platoon pressed against the side of the school building and I was on their tail with a skeleton headquarters. The school was a husk of brick with the whole roof blown off and shells screeching into it from the sky. More shells smashed into the road itself, into the orchard wall opposite, and into the orchard the other side. The road was metalled with no ditch and there was no cover anywhere. It was filled with fumes, dust and smoke. The blast was hot and acrid. There was a chaos of falling bricks, splintering trees and the nasty singing of shrapnel. Explosions were missing men by feet, and one would not have believed it possible to stay alive. Then the man two in front of me went down like a stone, face downwards in a heap, the rifle dropping from his nerveless hand to clatter across the back of his legs as he fell. The man directly in front of me turned back, his face ghastly and plastered with dust, and started gropingly to run, his wits shattered. Minds were too stunned by these awful few seconds for coherent thought, but the rear sections caught up and quickly the platoons were doubling ahead. The voices of the N.C.O.s could be heard shouting the men forward—"Keep moving, lads—come on!"— as they broke through the smoke and the wicked shells.

I had decided to install my headquarters in the white house. The stretcher-bearers had disappeared at the crossroads with wounded, and with the runners and signallers I threw myself at the door. It was barricaded. I hammered on it. Nothing happened. We all hammered. It was cautiously opened a couple of inches. A dark man wearing a corporal's stripes and the ribbon of the Africa Star with the "8" emblem peered through the crack. It turned out that the house was held by the remnants of a "C" Company platoon that had been left behind from the morning. The corporal survived as platoon commander. We tumbled inside. In the cellar the signallers desperately tried to get their set working, but they had stumbled with it during the rush and broken valves were found. This was bitter. Again we were out of touch with Battalion, and there could be no SOS calls to our artillery and mortars.

Meanwhile the shelling had become less concentrated, but was straddling the whole length of the road. Many houses were hit, and ruins shuddered with the force of explosions within. Across the fields enemy mortars opened up, and steeply down from the sky came the peculiar sibilance of descending bombs. The white house shook. The corporal with the Africa Star had no idea where any of our own troops were, and had presumed nobody else knew where he was. His men had been manning trenches outside during the morning, but had been blown out of them by terrible shelling. They had fled into the house, which the corporal had dourly prepared to defend until such time as a higher authority discovered him and told him to do something else. Sentries with bren guns were at various vantage holes in the walls and the rest were huddled apathetically down in the cellar. The corporal took me to an O.P. upstairs, where he showed me the remainder of the street. Detached houses continued for a further three or four hundred yards, with fields and trees on both sides, and the house clearing was going ahead doggedly, according to the "drill".

Then we went out into the open. He had his wits about him, this corporal: we snaked about trying to locate the enemy fire, and he gave me such information as he had been able to gather during the day. His former positions were across the road in a kitchen garden. Here, suddenly, we noticed a young Jock who had apparently been left behind. He was crouched against the side of a partly caved-in trench, with his head turned away from us. The corporal went to him and tapped him on the shoulder:

"It's all right now, laddie," he said gently. There was no answer. We had made a mistake.

"Poor kid," murmured the corporal with the Africa Star.

I started to contact the platoons. To cross the road from one to the other you had to go all the way back via covering sections at the white house each time, as the road was the killing ground. By degrees it appeared that the only occupants of the houses were enemy who had been killed in the morning. On the other hand, live ones were very distinctly out in the fields to our

162

flanks, shooting at us as we jinked and dodged along the backs of these forsaken houses. Even so, we could never be sure whether isolated groups or snipers were not holding out until each house had been searched. The work continued.

The art of street fighting was to see without being seen. The disadvantage usually lay with the attackers. Vicious bursts of spandau fire ripped across the back gardens and splayed into the doorways and windows of the houses. A man racing round the corner of a building heard warning shouts of "Look Out!" from his friends already inside, and as he dived through the door a stream of bullets streaked over his head, splattering into the wall the other side of the room at chest height, with the plaster and brick-dust flying. From somewhere out in the fields came the angry, snarling "brrrrrrrr!—brrp!—brrrrrr!" of the same bullets leaving the barrel of the weapon that had fired them, bullets that beat the speed of sound to be embedded in the brickwork beside you. Split seconds were the division between survival and oblivion, and to cross from point to point you picked up your life and ran with it. Sometimes it was the carefully aimed rifle-shot, cracking through a room like the lash of a heavy whip, and for a moment a stab of shock left you almost too weak to move. Or you climbed into an attic for a good O.P., then hurled yourself backwards, as with a hideous clatter of broken tiles streams of bullets pierced the roof, sprayed to and fro by the enemy machine-gunners. The living-rooms in the houses were a shambles. Broken crockery, nick-nacks, pictures and furniture strewn about, covered with dust and rubble. Yet—and time and again, as winter crept over the Netherlands, were we to notice the same thing—by strange chance the crucifixes and ubiquitous statuettes of Christ or Madonna and Child, encased in delicate glass covers, surveyed the damage quite unscathed.

Often, pinned in some macabre outshed or coal cellar, you found yourself crouching over the stiff features of a fallen enemy. Private Rawden, passing by, must prod at one of these

163

at the roadside with the toe of his boot: whereupon the corpse sprang to its feet and the hands flew to the grenades on its belt—it being an exceedingly alive young paratrooper who had been shamming for heaven knows how long. But for yells of "Quick, watch him!" from some of our men across the road we would have been another man down, and the astonished Rawden whipped round just in time with the point of his bayonet and took the youth prisoner. Then, because Rawden was like that, he gave his captive a cigarette. But others of more war-like disposition swiftly intervened and the offending cigarette was plucked away. The prisoner was subjected to a rough and ready interrogation which consisted of a persistent demand to know where his "Kamaraden" were, and how many of them. At first he stubbornly refused to say anything, then let fall the sullen news that a battalion of his "Kamaraden" were a short distance up the road.

By the time evening was approaching we had completed about three-quarters of our task, and our chances of being cut off and overwhelmed at dusk were only too good. It was essential to get in touch with the Battalion command post, so I started back for "B" Company to get at a wireless.

Now some of the heaviest shelling we had endured at Aart broke upon the bridgehead, from guns of big calibre, and obviously something was impending. The evil crossroads on the way to "B" Company were a hell again. I turned away my runner and ploughed back, and reached their headquarters. These were in some kind of timber yard off the road leading back to the church. A patient major called Meyrick had been commanding them since the days at Estry, and Meyrick and his entourage were all deep in trenches with enormous bundles of tall brushwood piled over them for head-cover, like wigwams. I found his signallers' wigwam and bolted into it. I seized the "18" set and bawled for "Sunray". Outside the wigwam cruel explosions were tearing up the ground. You could hardly hear yourself speak, but I got through the message and informed Giles about our situation. I was told to take up defensive positions, then to report back personally to the command post, and I put the mouthpiece down with trembling hands. The two "B" Company signallers were jammed side by side in the opposite corner of the dark trench, watching me. "Have a cigarette," said one of them, and I took it.

The bombardment was still falling when I eventually reported to the command post, which was in turmoil. Here I found more important events afoot than "A" Company's little battle. Tonight was the first stage of the relief. The reconnaissance parties of the relieving battalions were up, adding to the congestion and the place seemed full of C.O.s. And here was Giles. I was told a counter-attack was threatening, and to reoccupy "A" Company's normal area with my full strength. The men in the white house were to be sent back to their company, and after this I was to report to the command post again. The reason for the latter order being at Giles's side in the shape of a large and impassive major of the Argyll and Sutherland Highlanders, who had to be shown "B" Company area at the crossroads, as his company would be taking it over.

I was growing tired and frightened of that confounded crossroads, and started up the street once more, shamelessly quoting the Lord's Prayer whilst taking cover in a doorway, and got over the crossroads and back to my platoons. The platoon in the white house were sent on their way and I never saw their corporal again, and my own men were pulled back to the Company's regular perimeter. Eventually I deposited the impassive Argyll at "B" Company Headquarters.

Shortly after dark the attack came in, and down crashed our defensive barrages, and the enemy still could not reach us; at length came the familiar signals over our wireless network: "Enemy appear to be withdrawing."

The next night, after several thunderous hours from two more counter-attacks, Gordon Highlanders filed into "A" Company positions, and at last we filed out. For the last time stumbling over the corpses down the ghastly street to the canal, where canvas assault boats were waiting; and in the small hours, covered by the bren guns, we stealthily paddled across to the healthy side again, quietly, platoon by platoon, company by depleted company. Our responsibility was ended.

In two days' time the bridgehead was abandoned.

CHAPTER TWENTY-ONE

SECOND ARMY

THE Army was approaching the limit of the long pursuit. The impetus was running down. The last forward throw before winter closed in had begun. The Allied airborne fleets were out. Under Second Army operational command the great descent upon the waterways of the Netherlands had been made. The thrust to link up the airborne bridgeheads with the main weight of the ground forces was under way, but the enemy, hard upon the chaos of their defeat in Normandy, had managed to improvise a new front with baleful rapidity. The shuttle-service of German field-marshals to the command of Army Group "B" was capped by the return of von Rundstedt as Commander-in-Chief West. His still-plentiful forces were reacting viciously to this British shaft aimed at the Reich itself, and its red heart, the Ruhr. And at the sombre extremity of it all, Arnhem was resounding.

The airborne forces had dropped on 17th September. Meanwhile, east of Gheel, the Escaut had been forced, and under the Corps of the Black Boar, whose march had begun at Alamein, the vanguard of the main army drove forward. It crossed the Dutch frontier against strong opposition, and battled its way towards Eindhoven. Here a determined defence barred the way, but with American troops co-operating from the hithermost airborne zone, the town was carried. By the evening of 18th September the armoured spearheads had gained the Wilhelmina Canal at Zon, to find the enemy had blown the bridge while American paratroops were closing on it the day before. And it was during the early hours of 19th September when we came out of the Aart bridgehead back to Gheel.

Bad weather was now seriously hampering the airlift of supplies to Arnhem. But by dawn on 19th September a Bailey bridge was up at Zon and the spearheads were over. They reached the second airborne zone on the Willemsvaart Canal at Veghel, and the third, holding the Maas bridge at Grave, and linked up with the furthermost Americans at Nijmegen. The next day, 20th September, the great bridge there across the Waal, which was the Rhine main stream, had been carried intact against bitter resistance. A slender salient or corridor was now pierced up Holland, the forty miles onward from Eindhoven in places no wider than the single supply road that was its spine. At the height of the battle for the Waal bridge it was severed by a German battle group in the neighbourhood of Zon, but the belaboured Corps of the Black Boar, strung out from Eindhoven to Nijmegen, got it open again.

At the same time two flank corps were pushing up from the Escaut in an endeavour to widen the corridor and protect the vital supply axis. Increasing enemy resistance and the successive water lines made this a slow business.

In the 15th Scottish we were part of the left flank corps. Recuperation from our battle at Aart was short lived. On 20th September we moved from Gheel once more to the Escaut, where along much of its length the Germans still held an unbroken line, and took up holding positions.

By the following day the situation at Arnhem was one of crisis, and all efforts were directed towards the relief. We handed over to an armoured brigade on the Escaut. The perimeter at Aart was abandoned. In motor convoy we moved to a more rewarding crossing-place already secured, and thence in the wake of the Welsh Division into the salient. Late on a grey afternoon three or four graves and a blown-up scout car were passed in the ditch at a splintered frontier post, and further up, the eloquent wreck of an "Eighty-eight" pointed down the straight road to Belgium. Everything was totally flat. It was Holland. Far ahead the spearheads of the Army were beyond

Nijmegen. Within eight miles of Arnhem they were stopped by a violent anti-tank screen, dykes and mud; the Free Polish Paratroop Brigade was dropped and decimated; and the troops at Arnhem were cut off from the Neder Rhine at their backs.

We harboured for the night at the roadside south of Eindhoven. In front, 46 Highland Brigade, leading the Division, was already in contact with enemy beyond the Wilhelmina Canal at Best. The plan for the Division had been to strike for s'Hertogenbosch, some twenty miles north-west of Eindhoven, to protect the left face of the corridor. But this was not working out. Best, about six miles out of Eindhoven and only four miles from the main axis at the bridge of Zon, was in the way, and there 46 Brigade was held up.

Next day the Lowland Brigade moved up through Eindhoven, past the huge Philips radio works, battered by the R.A.F., into a concentration area. On the same day, above Nijmegen, the vanguard of the Army made renewed efforts: a little to the west of Arnhem, opposite the Oosterbeek woods, a column of tanks and infantry broke through, and the Black Boar had a foothold on the Neder Rhine. But the banks were too steep for the amphibious vehicles and all the river was under heavy enemy fire. Meanwhile, near Veghel, the corridor was again severed and numbers of supply vehicles on their way northwards were destroyed. This time twenty-four hours elapsed before the way could be forced open.

That afternoon our Battalion came under command of 46 Highland Brigade at Best to move into the attack. A Bailey bridge had been built and we went over the Wilhelmina and into a bridgehead gained by the Highlanders. Five days earlier American paratroops had dropped over this area, and from grim evidence in the neighbourhood of the Bailey and the blown road-bridge the enemy had been along the canal here in some force. Overrun guns and equipment were lying about everywhere, and enemy dead packed the ditches: the Yanks had certainly laid about them. A large wood near our start line had evidently been one of their rallying zones, and we moved through a mass of empty weapon-containers, ration cartons and the big white flutters of discarded parachutes.

Shortly before dusk our attack went in, delivered at a hamlet called Steenweg and a crossroads there, where the main road went north to s'Hertogenbosch. Steenweg straggled into Best to the left of the main road, the whole vicinity being a loose conglomeration of small market-gardens and a semi-urban residential area. Debouching from the woods, we made a long advance across wide flat fields under spandau fire.

Drawing close to its objective, "A" Company were enveloped in a violent smother of mortaring, and bringing up rear Headquarters as Second-in-Command again I had an alarming view of it. Denis of "B" Company, promoted a couple of days before to be Duncan's successor, was straight away among the casualties; his second wound, he had hardly had time, alas, to be Denis of "A" Company.

As for myself, it seemed my fate to survive, always to take over the Company at moments of maximum confusion; and confusion had never been more mystifying than here. I was now the only officer, and pounded forward to find about fifteen men warily creeping over a vegetable plot in the growing darkness, and the rest of the Company apparently disintegrated into thin air; and through the swirl of leaves, the spiteful echoes of random shells and the crackle of a cottage burning, one seemed to hear alien shouts and the dying clatter of other boots. By degrees the shaken Company came together, and dull, brute Dutch names loomed ahead of us. . . . De Vleut. . . . Donderdonk. . . . Boschkant. . . . and enemy in strength at Liempde; and the sleety fingers of oncoming winter came feeling through the dark woods.

Morning revealed the area grim with German and American dead besides some of our own. The Germans had a curious crop of fine watches on them, which quickly went, and unaccountable wads of German and Dutch paper money that, unluckily for those who thought their fortunes made, was found not to be valid Allied currency.

The Americans were a particularly unpleasant reminder of the airborne landings. Whole groups lay around their precious weapon-containers, surprised in the very act of arming themselves. Their attitudes, and the expressions on some of the faces, the precise moment of ambush transfixed in rigor mortis, gave these scenes a dreadful starkness. One G.I. had both hands shielding his face in a hopeless gesture of recoil, with a neat crimson bullet mark drilled through both palms and the centre of his forehead. A cottage had been a medical aid post: it was completely gutted by fire, but a board nailed by the entrance still proclaimed a smudged Red Cross. On the remains of a stretcher in front of the doorway were some charred bones and a purple, hairless skull.

There was some shelling, and here my runner, who had been like my shadow at Aart, was killed. He had been one of our Irish draft, and several times I was to pass his grave, alone at the roadside, where was ended one of those not widely understood phenomena—the professional ranker, with the certain leathery touch of his kind, and rather ginger hair, and goodness in him, who had served well past his term with the Colours. And one would think the world could ill-afford to lose him.

In the meantime stray prisoners were being rounded up. Two German-conscripted Poles were awaiting disposal at the roadside, with their countrymen forty miles away sacrificing themselves for the relief of Arnhem: for thus was the war. And once upon a time Monty had said it would end by Christmas. It was interesting to see if these two could corroborate this. . . . So they said the Germans could not win. There were not enough soldiers and aeroplanes, they said. Even the Nazis, they said, thought this. But the soldiers must fight on: there were men at their backs who would shoot them otherwise—and one wondered why it was better to be shot by us. They became expansive. If Hitler "Kaput" they said, all Germany "Kaput". Which led me to some rueful reflections, for we had all been hearing a good deal about Hitler lately. And when Christmas came along I wrote them down:

> Hitler's ill—and really bad,
> He doesn't speak because he's mad,
> He's just a myth: but 'pon my foot,
> I wish the beggar would "Kaput"!

Later in the morning there was a Battalion "O" Group. Today two Company battle groups were going out, "A" Company and "B" Company, with a troop of artillery on call to each, to clear some streets into Best and link up with the Glasgow Highlanders, who were heavily engaged. Giles said there were many Germans trying to get back to the Fatherland—which anyway served its purpose at the time—and that we were preventing them.

This time the enemy were inside the houses, and it took until evening to advance five hundred yards. Again we lost wireless contact with B.H.Q., far back near the canal. "B" Company, on our left, met with stiff resistance and the two companies were out of touch. Finally, from an O.P., various Germans were seen withdrawing over a railway embankment, but there was no trace of the Highlanders. The ensuing night was quite memorable. The Company never so short of officers and N.C.O.s as now, the platoons led by a lance-sergeant and two corporals respectively, but I still had the old sergeant-major. He went back for the rations to some remote collecting point across the Wilhelmina Canal and all sorts of things happened to him. By 5am he got the evening meal up.

Low in numbers, we sat out the night, barricaded into three or four villas in a tight defensive blob at a track junction, my headquarters in a tiny inner parlour without windows. A wireless message relayed from the supporting artillery troop gave warning of numbers of enemy beyond the railway, and in the middle of the night there was a stab of sten-gun fire outside, where one of the N.C.O.s, returning to his platoon from seeing me, had run into a small German patrol and pressed his trigger. The enemy made off, leaving two wounded, who were taken into Headquarters. One of them was a big, haughty, Prussian-looking fellow; a butcher from Rostock or somewhere. He was not badly hurt. He could speak a little English and demanded water. I had come in from outside:

"Tommy," he said to me, peremptorily, "close the door. I am cold."

All the while his companion lay howling. He had been hit in the stomach. I was on edge lest his howls would be heard by their comrades and our positions given away. I tried to get the big one to shut him up.

"Schweig!—schweig!" the big fellow muttered, but it was no use. Not prepared to risk losing our stretcher-bearers through having them evacuated all the way back, I had them carried to a house a short distance behind and left with some blankets until morning, but by morning the one who had howled was dead.

At daylight orders to move got through to us. The rest of the Lowland Brigade were now over the canal and a regiment of tanks from the Desert Rat Division had also moved up. There was a hectic plan to pass our Battalion ahead, northwards, riding on the backs of the tanks, which was cancelled because the tanks were needed elsewhere. At the same time a heavy counter-attack from the west developed against 46 Brigade. The woods to the north of us were also teeming with Germans, and the Lowland Brigade went into temporary defence. Soon our third brigade, from Aart, had come up, and the whole Division was deployed.

In pouring rain "A" Company found themselves back in their original positions at Steenweg, where the slit-trenches began filling up with water, and the next evening meal reached us at 3.30am.

It was now 24th September. During the afternoon the Army's main axis was cut again, between St Oedenrode, which was five miles north-east of us, and Veghel, where the enemy began building up a sizeable striking-force.

That night a trickle of infantry crossed the Neder Rhine but were unable to establish contact with our airborne troops.

At Steenweg during the same night I was woken by the sergeant-major with an urgent message, and dawn saw "A" Company, detached from the Battalion, trekking along the north bank of the Wilhelmina Canal to safeguard the Zon bridge, a few miles south of St Oedenrode. Arriving, we found a solitary member of the Dutch Underground on duty with a rifle.

Throughout the next day the Army was fighting to reopen the main axis, and the Germans now dominated all crossing sites on the Neder Rhine. The decision was taken to withdraw as much as possible of the Arnhem force under cover of night. The main Second Army vanguard struggled forward from its Nijmegen bridgehead, and the famous story came to its close. At night a battalion of the Dorsets broke across the Neder Rhine in assault boats, to face sacrifice as a rearguard and to cover the withdrawal, while some 2000 survivors came back across the river from the Oosterbeek woods, from the First, the valiant, Airborne Division.

A week or two later I was travelling in a truck up a one-way traffic circuit behind the lines. Around a bend and preceded by a jeep of "Redcaps" came a large car, travelling fast towards us the wrong way down the circuit in superb disregard of Provost regulations. On the bonnet a Union Jack. A passenger in the front seat beside the driver. In a twinkling an apparition—black beret with twin badges of Royal Tank Regiment and Field-Marshal, beaky nose and startling pair of eyes, and a face of great sternness—glared through my truck like a beam a yard in front of me, and was gone. "That was Monty!" I exclaimed, slightly shattered, to Private McKlintoch who was driving me. And mused what the thoughts could have been of the Commander-in-Chief.

The main axis was reopened after forty-eight hours, and lorries arrived to carry "A" Company, unassailed at Zon, back to the Battalion. The Brigade in the meantime had pushed further into the wooded area north of Steenweg. We handed over the protection of the bridge to a Light Ack-Ack battery and sped back. On the way we came upon the Divisional Commander, and I was signalled to stop. His jeep was at the side of the road, with an A.D.C. and a small escort, and there was the General, in balmoral and with immense cromach, an arm outstretched.

My vehicles pulled up. The General would speak with me. I hopped out and saluted mightily. In army boots I was a fair six feet, and barely over his shoulder.

Where had I been, and where was I going? I explained the Company's recent mission.

"Your Battalion got a bloody nose today," I was informed, in a gruff bass.

And with this hint, which I understood only too well, I returned to my truck and my small column proceeded. . . .

We filed into the Battalion sector. A dour atmosphere had been cast over everyone. There had been a vicious little affray. "D" Company, advancing to some miserable farm buildings, had been caught in the open by intense spandau fire and three parts destroyed.

The episode brought about the sole example of chivalry between the opposing sides in our experience of the campaign. The Medical Officer, collecting his orderlies, drove forward to get at the wounded in disarmed carriers flying Red Cross flags. Overshooting the mark, he ended up among the enemy. It appeared that they captured him, searched him, and took him blindfolded to a headquarters. He could speak good German and there asked permission to evacuate his wounded. Binding him in honour not to take advantage of what he saw of their dispositions, and giving him to understand that had we been the Russians it would have been otherwise, they allowed him to go free and carry out his task.

It happened that the following day a German attack against the "Royals" was cut to pieces under much the same circumstances, and a German emissary came forward under a white flag to ask if they might evacuate casualties and bury the dead, as had been granted to us. An hour's local truce was arranged for the purpose.

The heavy grey days passed. Days of local infiltration and counter-attack; perpetual stand-to; and artillery fire churning along drear tree-lines. Godforsaken tracks that led nowhere or anywhere. The snarl of the hidden spandau in a fir plantation. The strange voice in German sounding through a wood where the Divisional I.O. broadcast propaganda, and R.A.F. Typhoons circling in the sky. And lonely, derelict farms, and more dull names. . . . Gasthuishof. . . . Fratershof. . . . and some benighted buildings through the woods called Olland: for these names were now the work of the devil. And thoughts turned with persistence to when the relief might come.

For moral fatigue was on everyone. The strength was low. Replacements were not catching us up. There were not enough officers, nor enough N.C.O.s, and not enough Jocks. We had come a long way. There were many enemies. There had been no proper respite or refit since leaving England and it was so throughout the Division. In three months its casualties had reached a total of 7000 killed, wounded and missing.

It was so throughout the Army, and men were beginning to talk about the Army now. Caen to Arnhem had been the road, and the Army, men were saying, not without peculiar pride, was "played out".

But the Americans in their great numbers were spreading over the West, and soon it was being rumoured that still another United States Army was concentrating behind the Front, to carry the last phase of the war into Germany. Which did not work out quite like that.

September went out and the war carried on.

It was Nicht Kaput.

CHAPTER TWENTY-TWO

MAINLY SERGEANTS

WE were relieved by 51st Highland Division and went back to the Helmond area for a five-day rest period, which lengthened into three weeks. Here many casualty replacements arrived, and I handed over "A" Company to a brand-new major.

But, for a while, they had been my Company, and the N.C.O.s had been my right hand. And the story of "A" Company, or of any company, can scarcely be told without a word on sergeants.

I remember a scornful sergeant in a group of various sergeants exclaiming, "Christ! We're all sergeants here!" which was rather pulverizing, for he was a monumental and husky limb of the Highlands, in the Argyll and Sutherland Highlanders, whose dignity as a sergeant had been accidentally offended. "A man's a man for a' that," was this sergeant's outlook, which apparently in his regiment was played on the pipes when malefactors were marched before the colonel; and other sergeants called him Jock, and God help the Queen's enemies while his breed remain in these Isles.

I remember the wristwatch still ticking on a dead sergeant's arm in the Bois de l'Homme. "B" Company bellyaching after Hill 113, when all was reaction from the battle, and one of their sergeants wading into them so that they were scattered like chaff. And the huge, sombre sergeant long ago who administered to the Officers' Mess, and who told me where to put myself when I arrived, a trepidant second-lieutenant, for my first night in Ben's Battalion; he was later sent off the field by a games mistress for bad language when the Battalion hockey side played the Whitley Bay Girls' High School. I remember many sergeants. Sergeants who stood like the hills down the five and a half years of my army life.

The company commanders were the mainstays of a battalion, but its sergeants were its backbone. On the eve of the invasion of Normandy our Sergeants' Mess in Ben's Battalion was a superb body of men. Many of them pre-war Territorials, they were men clean-cut, who deserved respect. Nor did the sergeants who came as replacements let their tradition down. Since the first shock of officer casualties when we tramped through the cornfields towards the Odon there can seldom have been an action throughout the long trail to the Elbe without sergeants commanding many of the platoons. The lieutenants of the battlefield were so often sergeants, and the high casualties among officers was balanced by the amazing way the battle-tested sergeant seemed to survive action after action, to plod onward with the unlooked-for brunt of leadership upon him. Yet, sooner or later, even sergeants fell.

A peer among them was that unforgettable figure, Tam MacEwan. I can still see him, distributing haversack rations to my platoon on Hill 113.

"What's the ration, sarge?" they asked.

"Half a packet o' biscuits, three sweets and a bit o' cheese a man, and a tin o' marge for the lot o' ye's till tomorrow," came the answer, like an oracle.

And when I was promoted, Tam MacEwan led 7 Platoon down our milestones.

He was a year or two older than me, and for some eighteen months he had been my platoon sergeant. He was the kind of man whose advice one sought instinctively. He possessed an enormous fund of common sense, and, his advice sought, would screw his eyes a little, draw his head back and incline it slightly to one side and begin: "Well, sir, wouldn't it be better if. . . ." And invariably it would be better, much better. . . . He was about six feet in his socks, and beefy, with legs like hams and a large skull that he used devastatingly on the football field. He was a natural athlete. He played football, cricket and swam for the Battalion, and could have been a fine rugger player had he not been too devoted to his beloved "fitba'". With the Jocks he was always popular, for he was never vindictive or out of humour. They respected his judgment, and he gained their co-operation without shouting at them. There was a humane streak of reticence in him; he was slow to chide, and a tower of strength.

For three months Sergeant MacEwan and I fought the Germans together, from "A" Company. The question arose of his being commissioned in the Field. This had happened to a sergeant at B.H.Q. who blossomed overnight into Transport Officer. Duncan and I discussed it. His particular merits tended to make him over-slow to chide, said Duncan, when the need was for a harsher grip on his men: Duncan had just found muddy rifles in 7 Platoon. He should clearly be an officer and leave those things to sergeants, said I.

A bullet hit him on the nose while he was plugging bombs at a house with a Projectile Infantry Anti-Tank, in Best. The word spread round the Company that he had been evacuated, and it was everyone's loss. Corporal O'Shea of our famous Irish draft took over 7 Platoon. O'Shea, dark-eyed, unabashed and resourceful, looking up at me in the middle of Best and declaring: "I suppose, sir, I'll be going up to sergeant after this?"

And then big Duke, who got hit in the same hour as MacEwan, on the other side of the street. Duke, who with MacEwan had been with me when Duncan fell and had aided me through Aart. A rather older man, and very much a sergeant. The rank was his ceiling, and he was up to it with painstaking competence. Quiet-spoken for all his size, and even shy, yet a man of stubbornness and blunt with his words. He had a pride. It was well for the young officer to handle him with discretion.

He had come to my platoon in England as a lance-sergeant.

As soon as we went into battle I was uneasily conscious of a distinct personal animosity on his part towards myself, and could not think what it was all about. That awful first evening at St Manvieu he had stood in his trench with hands on hips, glowering at me. I was visiting his section, and when I was walking away he shouted something at me. Ages afterwards a wild solution struck me. When my patrol, of which he was the N.C.O., had captured the sniper in the cornfield that day, I kept the prisoner's Luger pistol. A little later I investigated how the thing worked by pointing it at the ground and firing it. A bullet barked into the earth about an inch from my big toe. Duke was there. Although only one man in the Company ever faced a Court of Inquiry on this count, who strangely enough was the Company "tough", the proverbial method for deserters to camouflage their intent was to put a self-inflicted wound into the foot. Could he have thought I was trying it?

However, the stresses of the campaign bore us on. From Estry onwards Duke found himself filling an officer's place at the head of 9 Platoon, and there he stayed. Periodically I was his O.C. and together we had to plan our battles. Fortunately his attitude changed.

Up the street in Best he was a big target. He came blundering back past me round the side of a house for medical help, his shoulder horribly drenched with blood. A strange rage and disappointment was in his soul. "The bastards!—The bastards!" he ground out, again and again, as he disappeared from my ken.

It was typical of big Duke.

. . . . Sufficient unto sergeants for a while. It is an October afternoon in Holland. There is a stir somewhere behind the lines. Along the grey kilometres men and traffic pull aside. "A" Company, returning to billets from a Mobile Bath Unit, halt in some uncertainty and face inwards in an impromptu lining of the route, carrying their bath towels. There is a flutter of Dutch civilians up the road. There comes a herald, in the garb of an Army despatch rider, wearing pure white equipment and with a big black-and-white check flag flying on his bike. At a steady pace follows a cluster of six more motorcyclists, all in purest white webbing, riding like superb bees on the swirl of their exhausts. Then a gap, then several jeeps swing by filled with Redcaps. Then more jeeps crammed with R.A.F. Police. A dark car appears, with a loudspeaker on its roof dramatically commanding all to make way. A hundred yards behind approaches the first of three purring limousines containing some Very Important People. The first draws level. There are two personages in the rear seat. Imperceptibly the sober kilometres have borrowed a moving dignity. . . . I throw my own salute. The man returning it, looking out in lively interest at a company of soldiers standing along his route with bath towels, was King George the Sixth.

CHAPTER TWENTY-THREE

THE YANKS

IN the hall of a large bank in Brussels the British pay authorities were installed down the one side and the American down the other. On the British side officers cashed money; on the American side most of the U.S. Army. But three will do: a trio propped one behind the other against the counter opposite. Immobile. Being kept waiting. A G.I. in a soft cap with the brim turned up, and an untidy battle-blouse unbuttoned to reveal a stark vest; an officer in peaked cap and neat brown service dress; and a negro in an overcoat and a steel helmet, oblivious of one another. Not a Goddam between them, but the negro as solemn as Judgment Day. The absent-minded rhythm of a jaw being the sole ripple in a tableau of inscrutable contemplation of the middle distance, as one of them chewed gum. Thinking of—who knows? They should have been cast for posterity, and inscribed: "The Americans, 1944."

We understood some of them became annoyed if we called them Yanks to their faces, which had something to do with the Civil War, but we called them Yanks among ourselves. And we all knew about General Patton.

Then, when we were at Helmond, operational instructions were issued for the assault crossing by 15th Scottish Division of a canal in south-east Holland, attacking towards Roermond through the American lines. This meant a move in great secrecy into the American battle sector.

Each battalion sent advance reconnaissance parties, and I was put in command of the party from Ben's Battalion. A U.S.

armoured division was holding the line here, in an infantry role. The line was static, along the canal, and for five days we lived among the Yanks in their forward positions. The vehicles in which we travelled had all British markings covered over, our battle-dresses were stripped of our formation signs, we discarded our British web equipment with its tell-tale outline, and we were given American steel helmets. In silhouette we were indistinguishable from Americans, and so far as the Germans were concerned we were Americans. And seldom have the Hollywood war films, with their guncotton blood-and-thunder, gross heroics and sentimentalized over-statements, even remotely recalled those Americans we saw at war.

The Americans we saw existed, like us, for small mercies and simple things. They lived for a smoke, the mail, the next relief, and—as the Dutch called it—for a lull in the "boom-boom". Emotionally, war to them was the same anticlimax that it was to us, and they existed as unheroically as our own men to get back home in one piece when it was all finished.

Like us—perhaps even more so, for as a nation they were less used to it—they disliked being shot at. There was also an absence of lusty soldiers' choruses: the Halls of Montezuma were in the film studios of the future, and far from gulping back the tears, the Yanks could obviously look at the Stars and Stripes without batting an eyelid. On the other hand, they were without the Briton's phlegm—and yet they had some of this too, and I think a brand of indifference of their own, best summarized by that useful expletive: "Goddam". Their humour was different, of course. Ours lay in the choice of moment in which to make a perfectly serious remark. Theirs was more designed for a laugh; to us, often, more corny. While, in spite of Hollywood, it may be we who are the more sentimental.

In an operational zone there seemed something vaguely incongruous about them. They had not shed their civilian identity to the same extent as we had: they did not go in for our conception of the "army type"; their military tradition had no parallel to our own; they were less used to wars. And there were many hundreds of thousands of them, and they possessed such a lot to give. It was not so much their hearts, but their generosity, that they wore on their sleeves.

Collectively they seemed fascinatingly youthful. The dour Anglo-Saxon stolidity and canny streak of the Celt was largely missing from them. They had "pep"; we probably had not their enthusiasms or the same kind of dash. And when they went forward in an advance or pursuit, with all their numbers and superb equipment, they certainly got moving.

Somehow, in the abstract, they invariably caused us to smile. There used to be wisecracks, too. But once among them it was impossible not to like them. Their friendliness was infectious, and in marked contrast to their group personality there was often a quietness, a touch of self-effacement, even of gentleness, about them individually. This, curiously blended with innocent enthusiasm for all things American and an eagerness to tell one all about it—disarming in its naïvety and complete lack of self-consciousness—tended to give them a charm all of their own.

In October 1944 it was rather thrilling to be "with the Americans". My party consisted of two other officers and some specially selected sergeants. There was a glimpse of the headquarters of the battalion to which we were attached, the steel helmets promptly encased us, and we were led away to one of the forward companies where we were to live. Our base was to be the company headquarters. This was quite a large set-up, with vehicles and tanks laagered about, and—we were astonished to find—some tents pitched. It was about half a mile or so from the canal. The land was dead flat, as everywhere, with several woods, although quite open closer to the canal itself. The Americans were holding a wide front and were decidedly thin on the ground, and the company had four platoon posts forward, each several hundred yards from the next. The tanks—Shermans or Grants—were laagered around them. A small road ran parallel to the canal and linked up all the posts, and a certain added thrill for us was that if you looked eastwards from a good vantage point, the top of a dairy building, or a windmill, your view stopped not a far march short of Germany. Down here, in fact, the nearest point on the German frontier was about ten miles away. But very great stealth prevailed. Especially on the German side, where a parachute division was opposing along this sector.

At the company H.Q. we were instantly overwhelmed with hospitality. Would we like "Tentage?" they at once wanted to know. We said yes, we would like Tentage very much: so two roomy khaki tents were erected for us. Lamps were provided. A stack of blankets was produced. These Yanks took their blankets into the foremost trenches and bedded down in them every night. If there was anything we boys wanted, just tell them, they said. We had conscientiously brought our own rations with us: could we use their cookhouse?—they had a mobile kitchen—we diffidently asked. Use their cookhouse?— why, come on up, they said, and would not hear of us eating our rations. Try theirs, they invited us. So we lived on their food and had tomato juice with our dinners and pineapple juice and waffles for breakfast, while they, inexplicably, fell upon our tins of stew and rice pudding and proclaimed them vastly superior to their own rations. We were also gratefully surprised to discover that they were sick to death of "K" rations. These, in their watertight casings, were like one-man picnics, and we slipped them into our pockets whenever we wanted a snack. It was also a novelty living on coffee, and good coffee, instead of tea. And of all these things there was an abundance. In the mornings, with the Germans half a mile away, a mobile canteen drove into the headquarters with "Cincinatti" or "Kansas" emblazoned on it, according to whichever home organization had supplied it, for elevenses. Back at the battalion headquarters there was a mobile cinema. Their entire administrative system made ours seem quite grindingly makeshift. At every meal two small bins on boilers appeared beside the kitchen lorry, one filled with boiling soapy water and the other with clear water, for washing mess tins. And we marvelled at all we saw.

Their more martial equipment was equally splendid, but their operational dealings with the enemy were a less happy matter. Although they were armour doing an unfamiliar job, there was nevertheless a fantastic state of affairs. They were supposed to be holding the canal, but there was no clear idea whether the enemy outposts were on the far side or across on the American side. It was our own small recce patrols, creeping about during the nights between the canal and the American lines, who confirmed that the German outposts were along the far bank. As it was, the enemy had established an unfortunate moral superiority. By day they kept quiet and it was extremely difficult to pick out any movement; but at night their patrols dominated the American lines with remarkable audacity.

The Yanks, to a large extent, had themselves to blame. There was constant movement between their positions, in full view of the canal, all day long. And whenever they moved for something they flew about in jeeps—which they called "Peeps". These Peeps shot about on the slightest pretexts—perhaps to say that there was another film show up—and the idea was that safety lay in speed. I got a lift in one. We tore up the narrow lateral road alongside the canal between two of the outposts, with the land as open as a billiard table. The driver was the cheeriest of souls; these Yanks were all the cheeriest of souls. "Don't you get shot up?" I asked. Waal, he guessed he just kept his foot down! . . . So the enemy had the positions taped, and each night we spent with this company a different platoon outpost was raided. A fighting patrol would come over, kill or wound a few men, fire bazookas at the dark tank silhouettes, bag a prisoner or two and make off again. There

187

were still a few stray Dutch civilians roaming about and viewed with suspicion by the Americans, who tried to round them up. One morning at one of the posts, after the nightly alarm, a Dutch girl came up to a couple of our sergeants who were there. "The Americans—very afraid!" she confided. A Yank near by who overheard this was not in the least put out. "Sure," was the equable reply, "we are afraid."

We had also to take the greatest care that the Yanks, in their now rather trigger-happy frame of mind, were accurately informed as to the routes our patrols took, and their timings; and for our part, that we had got the password correct. But on one surprising night our incoming patrol had to wake up an outpost, who were all bedded down in blankets in their foxholes, to tell them that we were back.

To the company headquarters, where something like a state of emergency was declared, the enemy patrols fortunately never penetrated. Occasionally during daytime the guns of the stationary tanks battered out in the direction of the canal, but when it was found that this drew enemy fire the company commander prudently clamped down on even that much offensive activity. . . . Certainly to look at he would have made quite a creditable Errol Flynn, this American company commander. He was a major, tall, dark and lean, visited his men in a waterproof blouse and dark brown slacks, booted, with an automatic carbine slung over his shoulder, and otherwise kept himself to himself in a small tent of his own. I rarely saw him except to co-ordinate my patrols: towards us he was correct and helpful, but one had the vague impression that he didn't like our faces much. Once or twice I went round his positions with him. "Mornin' boys," he would say. "Mornin' Major," they answered him, and it was all very pally. Finally the German night work was so troublesome that he gave a flat order to his men to shoot on sight anything that stirred in front of them. . . . "But what about the British boys?" they asked. . . ."You shoot first and aask questions aafterwards," said Errol Flynn.

All this time we were having some of those sharp blue days that October sometimes brings, and an impressive sight were the rapier-fine, silver-white batches of vapour trails, straight as fate across the skies, as every morning great clusters of U.S. Flying Fortresses thundered at a tremendous height across the German frontier. Never since the South Coast before D-Day had one seen anything like it, and on one morning we counted 500 Fortresses.

The same morning a wounded enemy paratroop sergeant was found at the roadside near one of the platoon posts. He had been a patrol leader, had apparently been lying up with his patrol there the whole of the previous day, and had been hit during the night raid by an American bullet. He was taken back to the battalion headquarters for medical attention and interrogation, and I went along too, in case he should divulge anything of use to us. The American army doctor spoke some German, and as he tended the man's wound he gently posed questions. But the prisoner's thin, haughty face never altered or gave a sign beyond corroborating what was in his paybook, and that he had served eight years in the German Army. Vividly one remembers the man lying there, on a stretcher by an open barn, and the American doctor kneeling beside him, a Red Cross painted on a white circle on his helmet, outlined against the clear sky. To every question the same reply: "Verstehe nicht." Why, softly insisted the American doctor, applying the bandages, must they go on fighting; what can they gain? And it was as if this doctor was speaking for humanity. But there was silence from the stretcher. The doctor tried again. Had not the wounded man heard of Churchill? . . . Roosevelt? . . . Eisenhower? . . . Montgomery? . . . The names of the Allied chieftains were dripped softly into the German's ear. And still the mutter was: "Verstehe nicht."

So the American doctor pointed upwards to the silver-white trails moving across the sky far above that barn, in the cold

189

sunlight. . . . The haughty face never moved a muscle, but the eyes were raised a moment, and slowly the answer came: "Verstehe."

Then the American Intelligence Officer brusquely arrived and the American I.O. was a German-born Jew. A flood of eloquent German was unloosed at the stretcher, ending with the subtle hint: would the prisoner prefer to be placed in the care of the French Red Cross, rather than face an interrogation? One gathered that the French Red Cross were rather rough in their treatment, and that the threat of them was apt to prove efficacious for the loosening of tongues. Humanity got a bit harsher.

The Yanks employed two expressions that cropped up with the frequency of the letter "e" in the English language: "Goldarned" and "Sunnuvabitch". What seemed to impress them above all were our bayonets. These were the standard British bayonet, a light six-inch steel prong with a good point, designed for the penetration of the human guts with maximum ease. "Gee," reflected a G.I. with awe, gingerly running his fingers up one of these, "that's a Sunnuvabitch thing." For our part, our vocabularies veered into new paths. We went about chewing gum from "K" rations, and one of our sergeants put the finishing touch when he appeared one morning with his stripes sewn upside down.

They would do anything to help us. The day before the main body of our Division were expected, a party of American engineers arrived, to check whether the enemy had booby-trapped a wood on the canal bank, which was a potential line of approach for the assault boats. Our own patrols had already been through the wood and had come across no booby-traps, and we were fairly certain there were none. However, the wood was pointed out to their officer, and in broad daylight his party had the doubtful pleasure of having to get to it and make sure.

As soon as they reached the wood there were bangs, and all

the little figures came tumbling out again. A few minutes later they were home within the outpost line, reporting that the place was booby-trapped. As a matter of fact they were being mortared, but they had hardly stopped to split such a hair. The officer came panting up to me. He was short and tubby, and a captain himself. As the senior British rank present, to him I evidently represented The British in my person.

He was not scared, it was simply the straightforward reaction that if there were bangs in a place the first thing to do was to get to hell out of it. And there had been bangs. So what did we want done about it? We British were the guys who had to do the attack. "We'll go back, Cap'n, if you say," said the tubby little engineer readily, panting away. And have gone back they would. I had only to say.

The panting little captain—"We'll go back, if you say"—perfectly represents the Americans, as we saw them, in 1944.

It only remains to be said that the forthcoming operation was suddenly cancelled. My party was recalled to Helmond.

CHAPTER TWENTY-FOUR

LIBERATION AGAIN

INSTEAD we were moved westwards, for a very different experience. This was to be part of the widespread operations aimed at clearing the Scheldt and south-west Holland, and at opening Antwerp.

At the end of the month we returned to our old battle area at Best. The whole enemy line pressing this flank had now fallen back, and we advanced to contact in the direction of the North Sea, across country that had been the German front line since the vanguards to Arnhem had first crossed the frontier more than a month earlier. It was a curious advance. Entire enemy gun-positions were left stranded, with the shells neatly stacked alongside. Mute "Eighty-eights" pointed skywards, their long slim barrels blindly aimed towards the former British positions at Best, their breech mechanisms destroyed. As we rolled up the defensive line of the Wilhelmina Canal, networks of empty trench systems were come upon. Scattered about everywhere were jettisoned equipment, and weathered traffic boards with their Gothic lettering, and all the litter of abandonment.

As the advance drew on, the countryside ahead gradually yielded a tall church spire, projecting like a needle beyond the intervening belts of woodland. At its feet a town of some 120,000 people—the largest town in the south of Holland except for Eindhoven, and our objective: Tilburg.

Some Dutch sources said the "Mufs", which was apparently the Dutch for "squareheads", were holding Tilburg. Others told us they had pulled out; and lone countryfolk waved their arms airily and said "Weg! . . . Weg! . . ." But we were

192

prepared to find the town defended in strength. Tilburg covered the German escape routes from the Scheldt.

Enemy rearguard activity remained slight, and consisted mainly of the delaying effects of blown bridges and the evil deployment of anti-tank mines, whose violent plumes of death took chance vehicles by surprise with stunning suddenness. It was our baptism of these.

At length our leading troops came within sight of the outskirts, and a formidable force of infantry and armour moved into readiness to attack the following day. Dusk came on, and by lamp and torchlight, weirdly slanting the shadows of men through strange barns, stables and stone-floored farm kitchens, the final conferences were held and the last briefings given. Beyond the woods and few remaining fields the slender spire of Tilburg reared into the darkness.

During the small hours patrols from the outpost line crept to the town's edge, crossing the canal that flanked the eastern boundary. Some of them were fired on, and lost little stabs of automatic fire distantly rattled the night, with the fate of a handful of men, somewhere, at stake. A few muffled explosions, demolitions or some nature of defence work, hollowly boomed through the stillness. . . . The enemy were within the gates.

Early in the morning the Lowland Brigade moved up to deliver the infantry attack. With a crash, the creeping barrage that was to take us to the edge of the town came down. From far back the heavier guns sent their salvoes erupting into strategic targets in the town itself and beyond. We emerged into the open. In the wake of each company clattered a covering troop of Churchills from the Guards Tank Brigade. In front, the irregular line of plunging shells; and we kept close, a hundred—fifty—yards behind. Warily we continued across field, fence and dyke, uneasy for signs of a reported minefield. We reached a canal and waded in. Icy water covered our waists, our shoulders, and men were swimming for it; and oaths were heard when a particular brand of tank arrived near by, ponderously lowered a good bridge from its back, and trundled over. We squelched forward, to within a few hundred yards of a row of houses, the beginning of Tilburg, but nothing stirred there. The bombardment had ceased and there was complete silence.

A road led to the houses ahead. The next moment some white flags cautiously appeared in the upper windows. Then more. They were being waved. Then the figure of a man came into view at the top of the road. He started to run down the road towards us. At first we thought him a German envoy conveying a surrender. Then he was seen to be a "Civvy". . . . On he came, straight for the leading section of "A" Company and fairly fell into them: a single Dutchman of Tilburg, beside himself with excitement. He gabbled his tidings, and had to be calmed. . . . The Germans had left the town! They left this morning on the other side of the town as soon as the British guns went "boom!—boom!" Yesterday they were in Tilburg, and during the night, with the people all the time waiting for the British to enter! Then the British guns go "boom!—boom!" and the "Mufs"—"Weg! weg!" Always the people have known that one day the British would come!

The dramatic news was passed back. The enemy had gone! But in case snipers and saboteurs were left behind, the infantry advance into the town centre was to continue according to plan.

As we reached the houses people ran out to wave. And more and more people. From every street they streamed, and ran towards us, cheering. Fortunately the guns had stopped before much serious damage was done, and such as had been wrought was chiefly confined to the roofs. Soon our route was densely crowded. They waved, they shouted, they laughed, and they wept. A shattering reception was gathering.

A halt was made by some open ground where we were supposed to dig-in; at least this was originally intended to be the first objective for "A" Company, and in the absence of orders to the contrary the digging was begun. But the shovels were snatched from the soldiers' hands as men and boys sprang to dig for them. A multitude collected round. The soldiers stood about, resigned and helpless. Unable to light up for a smoke without being rushed at by a small mob clamouring for cigarettes, or to take their rations from their haversacks without at once being besieged for chocolate and bully beef. For the people had not known these things. Black bread and potatoes, and five inferior cigarettes a month, had been their fare under the Occupation.

Soon Giles the C.O. arrived on the scene in a carrier, and rather a hectic Battalion "O" Group was held in the middle of the road, with hundreds of delighted townsfolk jostling them and noting their every gesture. Skittish young girls were soon miming this conclave of liberators, and trilled and laughed, and one of them came out with a startling rendering of the very accents of Giles the C.O. uttering his orders. Undismayed, the "O" Group persevered.

The upshot was that we were to push on to certain vital points in the town that would be guarded for the night. But all semblance of orderly movement became hopelessly lost. Tilburg was now a mass of wild humanity, and chaos swallowed us. The entire population must have been packed along our route. We entered the older part of the town, and all these delirious people still cheered and cheered. They showered fruit at us and storms of petals of the House of Orange. Men, young and old, ran up to shake us by the hand. Many stood at the kerb wringing the hand of every soldier who passed. Women with tears on their cheeks lifted little children to be kissed by "Tommy" as though the act were a dispensation that could formally dispel the shadows of tyranny. Some of our men had babies placed on their shoulders as they marched. The crowds had become so dense that we had to force a passageway through the crush, and one of our Companies reported over their wireless that progress was being made through "heavy civilian opposition". The whole way the soldiers were begged for autographs, and the ceaseless, incredulous question was: "You—real English?" But English or "Scottisch" it was all the same. "Tommy!—Tommy!" they shouted, and the cry in its way was this war with even greater truth than the battering guns to which we were accustomed. We were finally reduced to a state of moral exhaustion.

At last "A" Company reached their allotted area. But the Company Commander, myself, and the platoon commanders were unable to form the remotest plan among the swirling crowds. In desperation the five of us fled for sanctuary into the nearest house, where we tried to collect our wits and think straight. The crowds surged against the railings and even pursued us through a small forecourt to the doorstep. However, the owner of the house, who proved to be a local bank manager, quickly recovered from the pandemonium unleashed over his white hairs and rushed outside, tall and scraggy and flapping his arms about like an agitated bird, and shooed the crowds away. Then he came back to welcome with open arms the establishment of Company Headquarters in his home. "You are our friends!" he repeated at everything and to everyone. Later in the afternoon he managed to travel out of Tilburg the way our advance had come, to ascertain how his country villa had stood up to the process of liberation. Returning in the evening he tried to describe the convoys of vehicles and armour he had seen on the roads. But words failed the old man. He threw up his arms and could only exclaim, "Why— you are . . . mighty!"

That evening there was no billeting problem. The people of Tilburg roamed the streets inviting into their houses any soldier they could find. "We always knew you would come," they said. For when the British first entered Holland and Eindhoven was liberated, the "Mufs" had abandoned Tilburg. Then followed the Arnhem time, and the British were held in their

196

salient, and a long month dragged by. The "Mufs" returned to the town, and civilian evacuation was forbidden. Never had the Occupation been so ruthless. This morning, to the rumble of British guns, they had trundled away for the last time: on foot, by push-bike and farm cart, and by anything they could find. With our shells already spinning into the roof-tops the people had come out of their cellars and jeered and even now cartoons were appearing on the walls, showing the sight. . . . Then at the other side of the town, had come different men in other helmets and khaki. The Occupation was ended.

But triumph in Tilburg was short-lived. The following day we remained there, and around midnight an order flashed from Brigade placing us at immediate notice to move. There was an emergency elsewhere. The 15th Scottish were to be turned about. While operations had been in progress towards the sea, American troops, strung out along the eastern face of the salient in Holland and temporarily under the command of Second Army, had been the target for a disruptive adventure that had issued out of the grey flatness over the Deurne Canal on that flank. This had achieved complete surprise and the Americans at the point of impact had been overrun. Two Panzer divisions were advancing towards Helmond and Eindhoven to the heart of the communications of 21 Army Group.

We were rushed in motor convoy through the night. Before dawn our advance parties were being given assembly areas forward of Deurne village. Five miles westwards was Helmond. A few miles the other way was the Deurne Canal which the Panzers had crossed, and the chill wailing of "Nebelwerfers" and the din of battle, with a few British Units flung in as stopgaps alongside the American survivors, out there in the darkness. A confused medley of noise was stealing horribly closer. There were disturbing reports of Panzer spearheads two miles away, and all the way to Helmond bedraggled columns of civilian refugees were on the road. Locally, at any rate, everything was going back.

By daylight the main strength of the 15th Scottish was hastily gathering. We were thrown into the situation, with three brigades forward. Would the Germans come, an old woman trudging through Deurne asked me before we started?

We came into contact with the enemy in the next village. There was a battle, with Tiger tanks holding things up at a battered church, and I saw a young enemy tank commander, wounded and very pale, at the wayside. That night they brought the Luftwaffe over and we were bombed with shrapnel bombs.

The enemy were pushed back to another village, called Slot. This was ruined, for havoc had swept it both ways. The night before the Battalion attacked Slot, I was sitting in my trench in an inky wood, with the sand in my hair and rain falling, when a message ordered me to report to B.H.Q. It was my turn on the roster for forty-eight hours' leave in Brussels, and for Brussels I departed, and far away in a big hotel like paradise had my first hot bath in five months.

When I returned, Slot had been taken and a battle had been fought for the husk of another village, with every retrieved and shell-pocked mile marked with burnt-out American tanks and sombre little clusters of graves. It was a mournful reflection that these were from the same U.S. armoured division with whom some of us had lived before the plans were changed for Tilburg.

Then we went forward by infiltration at night, over pancake heathland, supported by a Vickers machine-gun battalion, and occupied various farmsteads on the edge of nowhere. The German advance was back where it had started, and now we were up against the canal on one side and a deep minebelt on the other: an utterly desolate stretch of country swept by machine-gun and shell and the sleet of winter. The fighting was bogged down to a standstill among mines, mud and marsh. A drear, spiteful existence of patrolling, gun duels and foray set in.

CHAPTER TWENTY-FIVE

THE PARTING OF THE WAYS

THERE were two lank, peaceable youths who maintained a quiet companionship and looked as if they should have been labelled, when the world slipped into catastrophe: "With Care. Unwarlike." But the world, alas, has a way of roping the unwarlike into its conflicts, so here they were in the Netherlands. In global war. One, who had celebrated his twentieth birthday by coming to Normandy, had once been an audit clerk not very far from Manchester. The other had been a clerk in Glasgow, and wore spectacles. Otherwise they were as alike as two bean-stalks: two gentle figures in khaki who roved our horizons with a stretcher between them, probably being shelled, and under the most startling circumstances doing their best very well.

They were sitting in the thick atmosphere of a rowdy, tobacco-filled barn on an October night before we advanced to Tilburg. It was the Company "smoker" at the end of the rest period, at which variety turns were being given by others of their comrades more gifted and vociferous in such directions; the proceedings generously lubricated by two or three barrels of beer, over which the sergeant-major, a stentorian M.C., was presiding, moist and happy.

These three I shall call Tom, Dick and Harry. They were all corporals in 7 Platoon, and inseparable. And they were providing several, it seemed, of the turns at the same "smoker".

Tom was a well-built lad, nineteen years old with a mop of tousled dark hair, whose speech indicated the Home Counties. Arriving in the Company before Normandy was over he soon earned a "lance-stripe", but a day or two ago Dick and Harry have been raised to two stripes, which has left Tom behind. So Tom asks for an interview with the new Company Commander. He knows he is young, says Tom doggedly, but he can handle men as well as any corporal can, sir, and is it right that he should have been passed over for promotion?

"Good for you, laddie!" was the answer, for the new Company Commander was vastly tickled. A man begging for more responsibility did not happen every day, and Tom was given his second stripe. Which was certainly one way of getting it.

Dick was about twenty-one and could have passed for sixteen, and possessed—to the delight of his audience—an effective flair for mimicry. Not very large, Nature had given him silken fair hair, blue eyes and a schoolboy *tout ensemble* that reminded one of old House Matches. But his home was Birmingham, and, an excellent young N.C.O. who had joined us before the Seine, he was presumably not so innocent as he looked.

Harry was the eldest. I was first conscious of Harry at Best. He was an alert, wiry little man who had served in the paratroops at one time, and was a North-countryman. He also nursed a remarkable dislike for Germans, and especially so on the battlefield, where men were often too preoccupied to worry much about it. But Harry harboured his bitterness, and his small frame quivered at sight or suspicion of his enemies. He hated Germans. It was his mission to kill them. He was like a terrier.

And when the beer had been finished, proceedings became a little confused at the "smoker". Rather incoherent songs were being shouted around a piano, in which anyone struck up. Suddenly, Tom, Dick and Harry were there, in the centre, holding forth with terrific energy. Their sergeant joined them. The shadows thrown into the deep recesses of the barn by the low light of hurricane lamps, cigarette ends glowing everywhere, figures seated about on the floor or perched on the high-piled bales of straw; beer fumes and fug, laughter, and the large group at the piano; and the three voices, joined by their sergeant's, for they were all pals:

Down in Arizona where the bad men are—
Nothin' else to guide you but the evenin' star—
The roughest, toughest, guy—by—far—
Is Ragtime Cowboy Joe.

So the campaign took us westwards and called us back eastwards. It was two weeks later when we came to the Deurne Canal.

The canal was on our left. The minefield extended from the canal at right angles; beyond it were woods, and beyond the woods was a sullen enemy strongpoint called Meijel. To the right, and past Meijel, miles of flat, bleak moor, peat bogs and marshland reached away. And this was the scene we stole upon by night. Twice-over a battleground, it was a Godforsaken part of Holland, sparsely populated at the best of times, with such few signs of civilization as there were almost totally destroyed and the inhabitants fled. We were also in uncomfortable proximity to a Panzer Grenadier regiment, among whom we had infiltrated. Both sides alternated amidst the dotted farmsteads or crofts, and any movement by day was dangerous. Every track was ranged, every solitary barn stood out a mile and drew shells. Even the cover of darkness was illuminated by numerous fires that blazed out of control and sizzled in the thin rain, started by the tracer that sped in all directions.

Here a Brigade attack on Meijel came through us. The attack failed on the minefield, but our forward Companies made a short advance to conform with the limited gains. This was little more than a walk from one battered croft to the next, past a few enemy corpses, and all was proceeding without incident when excited figures from one of our leading platoons were seen suddenly to run forward, to pull others in grey uniforms out of some trenches a short distance ahead. Eighteen apathetic members of the Wehrmacht were exposed and lined up with their hands above their heads. They had been found sitting in their trenches, fully armed, and apparently forsaken by anyone in authority. A corporal and a couple of men were quickly taking their identification and stripping them of weapons and equipment. This was where Harry came into it.

At the same time explosions and shouts were coming from a derelict farmhouse a little way to the flank, which the remainder of the platoon had gone on to search. Men were running and waving, and their voices came audibly across to us in Company Headquarters:

"Mines!"

The old cry sounded: "Stretcher-bearers! . . ."

A pair called McKay and Cripps went forward, but were nearly blown up themselves, and one of them was hurt. Men were now coming away from the farmhouse, some bearing wounded comrades, and among them was Dick, wounded in the legs, being carried out on Tom's broad shoulders. The next minute the platoon runner panted into Company H.Q. He reported the surroundings to the farmhouse to be heavily mined, and that there were many anti-personnel shrapnel mines. These were booby-trapped together so that one exploding would detonate a string of them.

Everything was happening fast. Volunteers from the next platoon immediately ran to the scene and several gave their lives in a rescue attempt. Others who were not blown up fell mauled. In their disregard for their own safety they had run on to more mines. A wireless call to B.H.Q. for Pioneer help had now been made. The situation was becoming unnerving, but the Pioneers were specially trained in mine clearance. In the meantime the plight of the badly hurt, lying around the

202

farmhouse beyond our reach, was urgent. I had called up the other pair of stretcher-bearers.

"You'll have to go over," I said. At least they could try to find a safe way. It was the one without spectacles who spoke: "What about the mines, sir?"

I remembered Tom among those who had come away unharmed, and told them to go to him. "Tell him to lead you in up the same route he came out by."

The same one spoke, almost in an aside: "Oh, well, we'll have to take a chance, I suppose." And they turned away with their stretcher and set off, joining the little group of men cautiously poking about on the edge of the mined area.

A few minutes later they were heading for the farmhouse led by the young yeoman figure of Tom. Shortly there were explosions. With instinctive dread I ran forward. A lank, bespectacled figure with a useless stretcher was crouching out there, lightly cut, and remaining rooted to the spot until effective help arrived. Tom and the other had had no chance. Their bodies had been seen thrown several feet into the air. It seemed strange that the day should still hold to its course, and for a moment you noticed the sky, and felt the slight wind. And the calendar leered that it was the Fifth of November.

Soon the first arrivals from the Pioneer platoon were coming up, with extra medical assistance. But the boobytraps defeated them, and more men were sacrificed. This killed off several of those they were trying to reach in a particularly dreadful manner. There was a man with his legs blown off, trying to stand up on his stumps. More of the Pioneers arrived, and their sergeant violently threw himself forward, prodding the earth with a bayonet to reach his own wounded men, until a mine blew up in his face. It had become a farce, played out in a world demented where inert shapes, horribly stilled under blankets, were retrieved as one by one the heavy stretchers were handled back.

As I looked on one of them a sort of clicking in the man's

mouth ceased, a sickening death-grin became fixed on his face. His eyeballs turned upwards into their sockets.

The sergeant-major, who had also seen, turned away briskly, looked at me, and vigorously shook his head: "No, sir. No, sir." There was nothing else to say.

Carriers from Support Company had to be employed to take away the wounded and the dying, and by this time a perturbed B.H.Q. had ordered the evil farmhouse to be left strictly alone for the Royal Engineers to deal with, who would fetch back the remaining bodies.

Later in the day a worried platoon sergeant was at Company H.Q. reporting his last corporal to be missing. We remembered that Harry had been told not to risk an escort for the bag of prisoners, since a good deal of scattered shelling was falling, but to let them find their own way to the P.O.W. cage. Either he had not heeded, or had gone out berserk on a one-man patrol to seek vengeance for his friends. . . . The answer was to come from B.H.Q. He had driven the prisoners all the way there, by himself, and a signaller had discovered his body along one of the tracks leading back to the Company; he had been killed by a stray shell.

They had buried him.

So he goes, singing ragtime music to his cattle. . . . The tune that brings back a barn, and the jumping shadows cast by hurricane lamps, and faces, faces of "A" Company, around an old piano; a dark October night outside, and a good way from Meijel. Inside, the singing, the beer fumes and fug. Forever associated with it on the crude verse of a song, a derelict farmhouse where the men must go. "Death House", they called it.

Finally, still later that day, a carrier towing up a gun from the anti-tank platoon. The noise of the carrier slewing round outside the battered cottage that was Company Headquarters. A violent crash, then silence broken by the sound of someone screaming. We rush upstairs from the cellar to be confronted on the doorstep by the sight of the carrier, tilted at a grotesque angle into a crater, its right track blown off. Hurled face downwards on the ground beside it a mangled thing, twitching, that had been the driver a moment ago.

The second driver still sitting in the back of the carrier with blood on his forehead, crying, crying his heart out.

CHAPTER TWENTY-SIX

JAMIE

A LARGE tin hat, tipped at an abnormal angle on the back of his head, surmounted his small person, like a monstrous and rather buffeted halo. This implied heavy weather. When the tin hat was up there was a battle on, and he looked at you quietly over the top of a hefty pair of ammunition pouches, resting on his rifle in a characteristic posture, waiting for the worst. Poor Jamie—he was particularly small and as quiet as a mouse, and really got considerably buffeted. Yet his might-have-been peaky features were relieved by the trace of that divine chisel which here and there touches the physiognomy of men. What whimsy, to have picked on Jamie who was so small! But there it was, and in slight surprise you found it dawning on you: a goodness there, of good structure, unobtrusive, yet curiously striking. And when he smiled—it was a rare smile—his whole nature brimmed into a pair of exceedingly light blue eyes.

Already glimpsed in the earlier days, he now departs from the scene, and cannot go unsung. It was at Death House, where nevertheless he was fortunate, and only as a "walking wounded" hobbled from our sight. And in Jamie, let it be said, went one more from that shrinking handful of Border Territorials, mobilized on that blaring Black Friday when the Germans marched into Poland and I was a schoolboy, to form our original Battalion. Besides, he used to be my batman.

For many months before we crossed the Channel, Jamie was my batman; he was a batman for most of his army service. He pressed trousers, polished buttons, sewed, collected washing, made beds, brought morning cups of tea and even

206

darned socks, impeccably; clean, discreet and obliging; ideal for the job. He was reticent of course, always, and devastatingly quiet, but something in his personality was worth cultivating; something honest through and through, and simple of heart.

He viewed one on the whole with tolerance, aiming a certain amount of mild but accurate humour at one's foibles. With some half-dozen years over me in age, he grew even a shade managing from time to time: it was part of our language. Officer and batman formed a sort of language which differed in each case. This was ours. And he wore a glengarry, and wrote immensely long letters home to his wife, and those were the good old days.

Then we went to war.

We arrived in Normandy. It was a rude transition and had a grievous effect upon Jamie. As I was a platoon commander his operational function was to be my orderly and personal runner at Platoon Headquarters. In theory at least he was still my batman, but the only "batting" of a kind that he was called to do was when we came back to a rest area, where he was supposed to look after my bed roll and keep my equipment together, because an officer had other things to look after. But alas, under the impact of battle and those hammering guns even this much burdened him. All initiative seemed to be draining from the once impeccable Jamie. With hideous infallibility he confused my kit. He tried, but could cope no more. I got irritated; these were nervy times and I think he was quite glad when we moved up to the line again. Our language totally broke down.

Day followed day: the hot, dusty, tramping days of Normandy; and his eyes grew unhappy. The smile had vanished now. His features became pinched, and periodically he would heave vast sighs. It was not that he displayed any "windiness"—far from it. Nothing seemed to shake him. Rather the resource was being battered from him, and there remained but apathy. He was simply carried to and fro by the surge of events.

He developed two tendencies. One was a tendency to sleep. Whenever he was not on the move, or doing his turn of sentry watch, he was sunk in the sleep of moral exhaustion. It was amazing that a man could sleep so much. Through the worst shelling, if not ordered to his feet for a stand-to, he would be at the bottom of the trench, oblivious to it all, asleep. Sometimes he would wake up and sigh a bit, then fall asleep again. All through the hell on Hill 113 this went on, opposite me. And the other tendency was to chew. He lived from meal to meal, and seemed to be possessed of some mysterious fund of biscuits with which to eke out the period of waiting for the next meal. Indeed, most of his waking moments appeared to be spent in chewing: a small, abject figure under the brim of that tin hat, pinched, long-suffering and needing a shave, whose jaws worked away, chewing. Opposite me. He had nothing to say for himself. He would not talk. Companionship, by a strange process of reversal, had been bludgeoned out by guns. Withdrawn in mute misery, he sat there in the trench, and still wrote to his wife—shorter, grubbier letters now, but frequent. Otherwise few thoughts could have passed through his head except for the periodic problem of how to shelter his little tommy-cooker from the wind when brewing-up. These we all used in the early days in the bridgehead, and with the cubes of dehydrated tea, milk and sugar, an excellent brew he certainly made. His tea capacity was enormous, and he hoarded his cubes and brewed-up whenever he had the chance.

So he existed. Poor Jamie. I must have been intolerable. A lot was sent to try us in Normandy, and for all the tea he made for both of us, Jamie, incessantly opposite me as we were semi-entombed together, from slit-trench to slit-trench, was becoming the last straw. Battered by the same Normandy as he, I muttered of these things to that mentor, Sergeant MacEwan, who tactfully looked wise. I even made a switch and had the platoon runner, a perkier man, in my trench, to avoid looking at Jamie. And all the months of our daily contact ended in a few heaped weeks of this. Yet there we were, under the kind of tradition that he was my batman. When I was promoted and went to Company Headquarters, I left him behind in 7 Platoon, unable to bear the sight of him any longer.

So Jamie became one of Sergeant MacEwan's henchmen and stayed on and on in 7 Platoon, surviving much and most of his friends, carried hither and thither wherever the path of the campaign led. I hardly spoke to him again; he was unobtrusive all the way, inconspicuous among the ranks of "A" Company. . . . Until at length you came across a small, rather unhappy figure standing by itself on the verges of Death House with its trousers blown to tatters. "You're lucky!" you said. He looked as if he felt anything but.

And thus departed Jamie.

But it was not the end. If, when the war in Europe was finished, you had passed, as I did, through the big barracks outside Edinburgh on your way out East, you would have espied a familiar small figure with a broom sweeping a landing in the Officers Mess there. You exclaim. He turns round and a pair of extremely light blue eyes go brimful with recognition. He leans on his broom with a rare smile. . . . Jamie, back at the old job, waiting for demob. Himself again, thank goodness.

CHAPTER TWENTY-SEVEN

NOVEMBER SCENES

A ND so to our Army in Holland. There a frozen-looking despatch rider standing by his motorbike, muffled in a long mackintosh, a balaclava and crash helmet, spits woodenly and with perfect abruptness into the muddy ditch. In a jeep plastered with all the heraldry of some heavy artillery regiment sit two dispassionate officers, side by side, in huge sheepskin jerkins with huge map-boards on their laps, who ought to have been on the cover of *Men Only*. In another place a mound in the mud of a road verge with a rifle stuck in it, and a German helmet dangling emptily over the butt. The burnt villages dotted back, the riddled church spires, and here a burnt-out tank with the whole turret knocked cleanly off and deposited some yards away by one frightful blow from a powerful gun. The miles of signal cable stretching rearwards through the slush. The ubiquitous Redcaps on traffic control at every churned crossroads. A German motorcyclist, mistaking his way, careers slap up the road to Deurne village into a column of our troops moving up to take their turn in the trenches, and crashes from his machine. Here a heavy lorry that has skidded into a ditch at a wild angle; the driver and his mate sitting near by, marooned on a petrol tin, chewing sandwiches. A crew from the Reconnaissance Regiment huddled in the shelter of a grey armoured car in their thick waterproof overalls, their goggles pushed up, brewing tea. The blinding flashes of the big guns at night, and the eerie, unwavering beams, far back, of Monty's Moonlight; and patrols, creeping over the marsh and dykes, cursing it at the skylines.

The new O.C. "A" Company sticks his face with glinting

spectacles in the top window of our croft to observe a spandau position. Instantly a vigilant shower of bullets rattled
through the roof—he swore afterwards that he had seen them
coming—and he spun from the ladder on which he was
standing and crashed to the floor, his finger snicked as though
by a penknife. For a moment I thought he was dead, and was
bending over him when another burst came through the tiles.
There was a tap where a bullet grazed a couple of inches from
my brain, leaving a slight dent in my steel helmet. Another
time a heavy German gun pinpointed us, and began to drop
enormous shells around Company Headquarters, ranging us
carefully. Craters were steadily torn up, slowly creeping closer,
until they were straddling us. Our croft was not strong. At
length we fled, and in the nick of time, tumbling from the
cellar with no dignity at all, map-cases flapping, wireless
headphones flying; the lot of us. The next two shells were direct
hits. The croft caved in on itself and the cellar ceiling gaped
at a smudgy November sky. The big gun stopped. . . . We had
thrown ourselves into a section of large concrete drain-
piping, conveniently half-buried in the kitchen garden by the
original civilian occupants of the place, to form a shelter against
the day when the war might sweep over them. It was
uncomfortable, dark, and you could barely stand upright, and
all curves—but safe. Inside there was a desperate smell, and a
Dutch family, who were in fact the rightful owners of the now-
destroyed croft. We bundled them and their personal
belongings, from food to pieces of furniture, on to the Company
carrier and evacuated them. The carrier looked like something
from a Chaplin reel, only not so funny. We then found it
necessary to empty our new abode of various utensils full of
excreta and urine. The family, with small children, had been
hiding there for about a fortnight.

There were a few clear days, but most of the time it was
raining, with mud and slush being mashed up everywhere and
the weather growing colder. Battalions were relieved for brief

rest spells as often as possible, and about once in ten days we went back to dry billets. But there was no relaxing of the intent of the armies. The idea was to force the enemy back to the line of the Maas, and towards the end of the month an offensive by other formations made a pincer movement across the Deurne Canal. Meijel was at last outflanked.

Our positions here became a back area. We could breathe again, and all we had to do was to get ready for the next demand upon us. And, as we were not in contact with the enemy, cookhouses were moved up to their respective companies.

"A" Company cookhouse has not yet been introduced into this tale. It had always followed us, though; a rather grubby mobile temple, its altar a belching petrol cooker; for everybody knows that an army marches on its stomach. And if you took any farm stable, any barn, any shed, garage or yard, any field— but a sheltered spot, any accessible corner with or without a roof that offered some protection from the elements, there you might find it. In any place, from the beaches of Normandy and paddocks of the *bocage*, over the rolling lands of Northern France, neat Belgium, these canals and dykes and flat wastes of the Netherlands, and onward to the wooded Rhineland, the heaths, forests and undulating vistas of the North German plains, even unto the shores of the Baltic . . . stewing, boiling and baking its way across Europe on the heels of the fighting, and scattering in its wake a long, long trail of tins. Tins of all shapes and sizes, from "A" Company cookhouse.

King-pin, in other words Cook, was "Dusty". Dusty was economically built, sandy-haired, blue-eyed, from the Edinburgh direction, and difficult. Dusty was laconic and terribly Scottish. Dusty could extract the bully beef from a tin in about two deft movements—he punctured a hole in the base and blew. He was kind to undernourished civilians, fed stray children, was canny, smart when he tried, and could harbour a grudge. Dusty could cook excellently or be indolent, as the mood took him. He responded to praise. He had to be wooed.

Another, deeper denizen of the cookhouse was a savage soldier called MacTavish. MacTavish did not speak. He grunted, and never wore teeth. The appearance of MacTavish was bellicose, although I never saw him actually slay anyone. This appearance may have been due to the shape of his jowl and skull, that looked of enormous thickness. He lived in soiled canvas trousers and a ferocious singlet, and was Assistant Cook. If addressed directly he would jerk his head in swift affirmative and might, or might not, grunt. And the cookhouse travelled about on the wheels of our three-tonner lorry, driven by a resourceful soldier of uncertain humour called Private Gillies, a Border Scot and pretty tough, who had been with "A" Company since the year dot. What Private Gillies was thinking was nobody's business. Although quite young, he was an old hand, and he lent it to the cookhouse, where he was cheek by jowl with Dusty—and MacTavish.

The cookhouse fed "A" Company with an invariable hint of slight reluctance, as though it were barely compatible with their dignity. The cookhouse threw temperaments like a ballet chorus. The cookhouse was a brotherhood—a priesthood—apart. Only a few other characters were admitted, like select moths, into the light of its hurricane lamps: such as the ample figure of Private Bates, Company storeman, whose tongue had grown sharp in the course of office, various other drivers like Private Wheeler and Private McKlintoch, and one or two favoured sick or left-out-of-battles, who were roped in to do the chores and allowed to hang about for extra food.

But supreme over the cookhouse scene there brooded the figure of the colour-sergeant. . . . We had a colour-sergeant. One who arrived when Macbain left us. He was an implacable man. A big Londoner, fresh faced, useful on the football field, and as temperamental as a prima donna. On many administrative matters concerning "A" Company he was answerable to me, as Second-in-Command, and within the larger war that was being fought across Europe there existed a perpetual minor state of warfare between the colour-sergeant and myself. Our only armistices were when I was commanding the Company; but afterwards, inevitably, our hostilities would break out anew. He was a man of character, clear wits and authority who knew his job. He had good manners; could put on charm. He could come "the old soldier", or put paid to it in others. And he knew his own interests, and how to pursue them. That was the trouble. He had many faces; I could never get to the end of them. That colour-sergeant defeated me. He probably only needed someone mature enough to be firm with him, but there he was, large and implacable, not a bad man, brooding over the cookhouse. . . .

Here passes across the scene the man of whom it is fair to say: He Knew No Fear. It was not that he was ignorant of the meaning of fear, for he was no fool, but simply that he used to experience none. Admittedly, the sergeant of 7 Platoon, Tam MacEwan's successor, was fearless in a sense; in that determination—or call it guts—could exclude other emotions. It had been so with Corporal Harry for that matter, but at least they knew apprehension. With this man—no.

He was a peacetime soldier who had served in India with our 2nd Battalion and came to "A" Company before we left England, with two stripes and a medal and a rough reputation, and the improbable name of Whitemark. But home life did not suit him. He was a tricky customer.

When we went to Normandy he was posted to another company. In the Netherlands he was posted back to us. He was a sergeant now. In November he was commanding 9 Platoon. For put this man in a battle and he was transformed. He emerged a leader, and his men followed a calm, ruthless personality who appeared to relish killing and had personally accounted for many of our enemies. He volunteered for patrols. Stray chickens, rabbits, duck and on at least one occasion a luckless piglet mysteriously supplemented his platoon's rations

214

when this astonishing person was around. His resource was unbounded. He knew no law. The battlefield was his element.

He had a dry humour, a cynical attitude to the events he came up against, and apparently no post-war aspirations whatever. In moments of strain or danger he was the finest of companions. What went on inside the mind remained an enigma.

Once I asked him why he enjoyed the kind of life we were leading.

"Ah, sir," was the answer, "I'm a nomadic type."

With the Meijel area no longer a forward zone, there were some liaisons with the Guards Tank Brigade, and a few of our officers were sent to them in rotation for short visits.

The Guards Tanks were recuperating and doing maintenance at Helmond at this time. One arrived at the squadron of Grenadiers that supported our Battalion in the middle of a flurry of drill parades. Words of command rang. Subaltern officers, dumped in the ranks with their men, were being drilled by their own sergeants, and squads of Guardsmen in canvas dress and berets were being vigorously marched and counter-marched on all sides. One reported to the squadron commander, a big, fair, cheery man of about thirty with an Africa ribbon on his breast, who at once took the reasonable view that these visits should be more in the nature of a holiday for us infantry people. This arrangement was fine, and one was free to drift about as one liked and to relax.

I lived as a guest in the squadron Mess, and was soon being denuded of every possession with alarming speed at strip poker. From this I was aptly rescued by the infantry liaison officer, of whom there was one in each squadron. He was a captain, very tall, lean, dark, and had a somewhat sallow face that was extremely good-looking, with sardonic brown eyes, moulded cheekbones, a strong, finely drawn mouth and a perfect nose, and a wit that dropped with mocking bite from bloodless lips.

They were not all like him, even from Eton and the Guards; but he, indeed, should be in a book. His time seemed to be spent in an entertaining quarrel with the squadron second-in-command, who was quieter and less typed than the others, and a good foil.

Completing their Mess were four troop leaders. One of them was a solid, good-natured, mature fellow with a large black moustache who only uttered in the broadest Yorkshire accent. At first I was horrified: but I need not have worried, he just enjoyed doing it. Another was the inevitable Honourable, uninteresting, who casually drifted in and out, obsessed by swing music. At intervals he captured some on the wireless and they all had a jam session, and jigged. Then there was an impetuous youth with feminine turns of phrase and a happy brand of appalling manners who was the constant butt of everybody's wit. Being no doubt used to that sort of thing from an early age, the end of his nose merely twitched in practised good temper when they teased him; his obsession was food and at every meal he had his greed explained to him in a number of original ways. And lastly there was a pretty, blond child, who might have stepped straight from his House Cricket XI, and was known as Julian. . . . "Really," murmured my rescuer from the poker game, with an eye on the usual target, "I sometimes wonder if its Julian or Julia." And they all called him "boy" and made him fag for them.

Over this gathering the big squadron commander cheerfully presided, and one knew ever so surely that his word was the law. He had recently caused a few dozen cases of port to be laid down as a christening present to his son and heir, for the day when the infant could be initiated by the judicious parent. He spoke with eager deliberation, this squadron commander, and here, one felt, was a man who loved living.

These Guards were big men in big tanks. In action they moved with the measured caution and unagility that bigness seems to entail. Their officers were amusing to walk around

216

with: they walked with massive tread, even the quite small ones, even the boy, as if from sheer parade-ground force of habit. I was also allowed to play about in the tank park, and here were all the Churchills. The crews and specialists swarmed over them, at their maintenance, and in all these monstrous hunks of mechanism the one piece that was kept so well greased and spotless that several inches of solid steel swung open at the touch of your little finger was the emergency escape hatch beside the driver's seat.

For instructional purposes I was placed in the boy's care. He took me out for a spin in his Churchill, and while we were out they let me take over the controls. I squeezed into the driver's place with the headphones over me, and for a mile down a straight road drove the forty-odd tons of armour that comprised that famous tank. Halfway along there was a twist in the road where we crossed a narrow Bailey bridge over a canal. In spite of the crackling headphones and my attention being riveted on the driver's view aperture, I sensed a distinct stiffening on the part of the crew as we approached it. The boy, up in the turret, hardly dared tell me anything through the intercomm. They had not catered for my enthusiasm running away with them.

At Helmond an enemy jet aircraft came marauding over. The Germans made early use of these. It was hit by an Ack-Ack shell from one of the batteries: the big black shape suspended for an instant in the sky, in a death slew, to fall away behind the house-tops.

CHAPTER TWENTY-EIGHT

CHRISTMAS AT VENLO

A T the beginning of December our Brigade assaulted the last German stronghold west of the Maas, at Blerick-Venlo.

More than two centuries ago, when Marlborough laid siege to the old fortresses of the Maas, the key position of the Venlo defences was an earthwork on the west bank where Blerick stands today. Here again there was a fortress, and the small town of Blerick, a salient in a bend of the Maas, lay behind a two-mile perimeter of minefields, barbed wire, trenches and strongpoints, and a deep anti-tank ditch, all covered by a large number of enemy guns and mortars on the Venlo side of the river.

The assault, swiftly following a deception plan, achieved a large measure of surprise, and was supported by 400 guns, rockets—that had never been used before on land—and an Armoured Group and breaching force. The entire Brigade were carried to their objectives in armoured personnel carriers, like tanks without turrets, called "Kangaroos", each sheltering up to a dozen men, and the operation was such a success that it became the subject of a War Office pamphlet.

In "A" Company we sailed into Blerick virtually unopposed. The Company had passed under still another O.C., an astounding character called Basil, in whom past experience as an air liaison officer had effected a markedly R.A.F. touch; and immediately we "depouched" from the Kangaroos on the edge of the town, an agonized "Get me out of here, old boy" announced to me that Basil had unluckily been hit. He was our only casualty.

Mopping up continued until we gained the riverside, screened by a smoke barrage from the stunned façade of Venlo and the remainder of the Germans opposite. And as we trod over the rubble in the streets of Blerick that evening, faces peered out at us from cellars and doorways, as shaken remnants of the civilian population, who had never been evacuated, cautiously made their presence known and called "Tommy!" as we passed. They seemed to think we had set them free. Arrangements were quickly made to evacuate them, and before long they were collected and moved out by night. The little town, gaunt and ghostly, cleared for stealth and the shells.

The Ardennes counter-offensive shortly caused the disappearance of various British divisions to Belgium, to cover the Meuse crossings in the American rear. The Divisions remaining in the Netherlands to keep vigil on the Maas, on an already wide front, were now left with precariously little at their backs. Our Brigade frontage in the Blerick sector was the almost impossible distance of eleven miles, and this was held by two battalions, one of which had to be kept in Blerick itself, and a solitary squadron from the Reconnaissance Regiment. The third battalion was in reserve five miles behind.

Our own Battalion held Blerick. The Maas was broad, and swollen by the winter rain, although often at night on the waterside you could hear German voices shouting, across in the larger town of Venlo. But it was really one place, where the tall houses faced each other across the river, Venlo on the east bank and Blerick on the west bank, and the Maas between. A big bridge carried a main-line railway to Essen and the Ruhr, only there were no trains when we were there and the broken back of the bridge sagged ponderously into the grey river in a mass of twisted girders. A few thousand yards beyond the Venlo roof-tops rose the low sombre outline of Germany.

On the enemy side highly aggressive parachute troops had been moved up. They combined an extraordinary bravado—

even revelry occasionally sounded from Venlo after dark—with great cunning. Our role was to sit tight, and patrolling was deliberately shut down, but on many nights there were reports of their patrols on our side, although the river was a formidable obstacle. They crossed in small boats, operating with the audacity one had learnt to expect from these paratroop formations and some of them performed amazing feats. It was soon the fastness of the winter, with snow and bitter weather; but one patrol, on a January night with the temperature below zero, had actually swum over. Another surprised an outpost of the Recce Regiment and "kidnapped" the lot. And one morning above a house on the Blerick waterfront a healthy Swastika flag was observed to be flying. Unfortunately the house was covered by enemy fire and could not be reached in daylight, so for the time being the flag had to remain, and rather embarrassingly flew over our Battalion area for the rest of the day.

For a month we remained in Blerick in our barricaded strongpoints among the battered, spectral streets. It was a peculiar kind of life. We were in the shadow of the Fatherland. The physical presence of the frontier entered the very cellars of Blerick. It was not fifty miles from the Ruhr, and sometimes at night there was a distant murmur of bombers, and air-raid sirens could clearly be heard wailing in the Rhineland.

By day there was little movement, and a pall of mystery and quiescence hung over the river, broken only by the spasmodic crash of projectiles. Sometimes one side started a concentrated artillery or mortar strafe, which instantly provoked reprisals. And at night the defence work and supply, on both sides, took place. Venlo, especially, sprang to life. Banging was liable to break out all over the town, stakes would be hammered on the river bank, a particular concrete works invariably rang with sound, while traffic, possibly moving down to the Ardennes, could be heard in the distance. We sent up parachute flares and had bren gun shoots, and, in all, we more than held our own in the throwing of lead across the Maas. Then one day we were bombarded with leaflet shells. These, printed in English, regretted that we were not home for Christmas after all, and declared that any British soldier who dared the crossing of the "Meuse" would never reach the far bank alive: the Meuse, we were informed, would turn red with our blood and wash it back to the cliffs of Dover. At the foot of the sheet was:

Death in the Meuse!
Death in the Meuse!!
DEATH IN THE MEUSE!!!

Each company and even platoon area, effectively isolated by intervening buildings, was its own world.

In "A" Company Headquarters in Pepijnstraat we were well settled. It was a little red brick house, knocked about upstairs but little damaged on the ground floor, where we all dwelt. The windows were covered by wire netting against grenades from possible enemy patrols, and there was a good cellar. Here I established our command post, with a new sergeant-major. With his predecessor there seemed to have gone two eventful, very long years of my life, the last of New Year's Eve 1943-44, and a part of "A" Company; and, sole survivor of the old regime, I missed him.

There was also, for the short while before the civilians were sent away, the family who belonged to this house. They existed in a communal shelter near by, where about fifty people had taken refuge, but still came in to use the kitchen: a middle-aged man and wife, whose eldest son had been taken for forced labour into Germany, and two younger boys—of whom the smaller, called Rikky, became unreservedly attached to us. Two years afterwards I had a letter from Rikky: "Here in Blerick the same except that our house isn't repaired hitherto, but there are so much people that lives in a hen house so that we mustn't complain."

221

Rikky was sixteen. He told us how he and the other youths of Blerick had been marched out by the Germans to work on the anti-tank ditch. There in the corner was the new Wehrmacht helmet they had given him. He told us how the morning of our attack the "Green Police" were going to parade all the remaining males in a final forced-labour round-up and Rikky was very thrilled that the British had come. . . . He played the accordion. For hours he sat with us, and played to us. One of our favourites, that the Germans used to sing when they were in Blerick, was "Fatherland Your Stars", "Heimat Deine Sterne"; and it was certainly a haunting tune, there in Blerick-Venlo, with those wailing sirens far out in the Rhineland, and the stars themselves were the frontier. And not least he played that tune of the Second World War, of the soldier's dream lady, inevitably waiting by the lamplight: "Lili Marlene."

Poor Rikky. He was so eager; and when he had to leave us he was really sad.

Hard opposite were the headquarters of 8 Platoon. And there, in a domain of their own round the back, would sit one Larry, a new Canadian platoon officer, and his sergeant, the veteran, bear-like "Gibb", who had survived all this way. Talking far into the nights. Yarning and yarning at a kitchen table, the two of them: at least Larry doing most of it. Larry in his sleepy drawl, telling "Gibb" about the Rocky Moun'ns and all sorts of wonderful things, home in Canada. Larry drawling from seaboard to seaboard, and "Gibb", who has known but a Border farmstead and perhaps the odd bucolic spree to Edinburgh, but not unwise for all that, solemnly puffs at that ancient pipe we knew so well in "A" Company, with its tin cover and the three percolated holes, and says, "Oh, ay," at intervals, with immeasurable comprehension.

Down "mortar-bomb alley", with the jink in it the enemy had so well ranged, you came out on the broad stealthy street with the big fallen trees, along the river. Here the enemy probed for our forward positions with high-velocity guns over open sights. Immediately opposite the mouth of the alley, in a big battered white house, was 7 Platoon, and straight across the river rose the spire of Venlo's old church, with daylight through it. The Germans used it as an O.P., and one of our anti-tank guns at maximum elevation tried to knock it down one morning, but the spire never fell. In front of the big white house was a garden, and following a communication trench you came to a forward section in a small bungalow—a kind of summerhouse. Inside was a bomb-plastered shambles and a little passage, and at the end of the passage was a door. If you had opened it and gone outside you would have fallen into the river, and in the door, on an exact level with the crutch of a man standing behind it, was a bullet hole. This was somehow the most horrible bullet hole in Blerick; and that door was the frontier. . . .

Further along was a pleasant house in another garden that had obviously belonged to well-to-do people and was now occupied among a lot of rather sad-looking destruction by some of 9 Platoon. In one of the rooms was a set of revolting photographs of a man and woman murdered in their bed, and in some of the photos the frontier stood in black uniform against a light window, the face indistinct, holding a tommy-gun. . . .

On across a gap by a disused ferry site with a stark view of the river at your elbow, so for ten yards you sprint for it, and you come to some high buildings occupied by more of our men. And here, from the top windows, the frontier was constant: that ordinary line of high ground against the dull white sky, half an hour's walk beyond Venlo.

And all this time tiredness was creeping in. You went round in the nights, touring the posts, with two men and a bren gun as escort, your feet swathed in sandbags in the silent streets, and bleary-eyed corporals unbarred doors, and the heavy silhouettes of sentries, sitting out the hours of darkness at blank windows overlooking the river, dutifully stirred. While on other occasions their equally tired company commander at some ungodly a.m. would find all wrapped in abysmal slumber. This was the cardinal sin. Nor was that all, for living in houses had its relaxing effect: carelessness in defence work and at concealment had to be checked; and the German, sometimes to our cost, was the more industrious.

Then came the Christmas "flap".

The theory was that the Germans were coming across the Maas in strength on Christmas Day. Prisoners taken on the river further south disclosed that they were having their Christmas dinners early in order to be ready to attack across the river on Christmas night, and it all lent drama to the season. There were many rumours, and an intense watch was kept for signs of the enemy bringing up assault boats and bridge equipment. There was also, throughout all this period, a steady trickle of courageous Dutchmen who got through the German outposts and across the Maas at night to us by ingenious means, bringing with them information of varying reliability, and from a civilian source shortly before Christmas it was reported that two thousand fresh paratroops had been moved behind Venlo in readiness for a foray.

A state of emergency was declared. The Germans certainly began their celebrations early, and a couple of days before Christmas merriment waxed in Venlo, intermingled with the laughter of women. At night a distant brass band was heard, and on Christmas Eve church bells were ringing from a village a few miles up the river. Familiar carols, and the strains of "Stille Nacht", came stealing over the Maas.

The great day arrived. In the small hours some more Dutchmen got across and said the Germans were all drunk, an encouragement to their condition apparently being their impression that at Christmas the British always got drunk. And there were no signs of an attack, said the Dutchmen. So the 25th dawned quietly, a perfect snow scene, and promising a complete anti-climax.

But there was little brotherly love lost between the banks of the Maas. "Come across and fight, you Scotch bastards!" shouted raucous German voices in English at the forward posts of the "Royals", while Ben's Battalion in Blerick had no intention of being caught out. Christmas dinners were eaten at midday, and thereafter alcohol was forbidden; but if the Germans thought this Battalion were drunk, let them. Accordingly, after dark, the Regimental Sergeant-Major arranged for large bonfires to burst forth behind the town, as though drunken Britons were setting houses alight, and from Battalion Headquarters an improvised band struck up. From each Company in turn more fires were lit and Noise Parties, carefully simulating Bacchic orgy, rent the night. The rest of the Battalion were lining the river with their fingers on the trigger, hoping the enemy would be tempted across and be slain. The result was an enormous flop. It was the one night when somnolence reigned in Venlo.

After Christmas the Battalion were relieved, for a day or two in reserve, then returned to the forward positions for three weeks of an icy January; quite houseless this time, along the open river in the snow. Eventually, after seven weeks of keeping watch on the Maas, the Brigade moved down to Belgium to be rested.

We went into winter quarters in a small town about twenty miles from Brussels. But events were moving now. The Ardennes threat had been defeated, and great and secret things were afoot. The battle for Germany was on every horizon. Within a week we were rudely off again, and the convoys slipped and skidded over the ice-covered roads back into Holland, to a familiar billet in Tilburg, where 15th Scottish Division were all concentrating.

Tilburg had become a large base and the Headquarters of Canadian First Army. It was a time of fleeting, sharp blue skies and frosty sunshine, of flying-bombs chugging overhead for

Brussels, or the coast, of rumours of V2 vapour trails vanishing at their terrible altitudes; and of mighty prelude.

Earlier in the month the great Russian offensive had begun, and some comic said the Red Army had burst through at Nijmegen and that we were going up to counter-attack.

CHAPTER TWENTY-NINE

A CONVERSATION

OVER the New Year I was in hospital with jaundice. On New Year's Day a Luftwaffe pilot who had been shot down was brought into the next ward, and hearing that the formation badges of his escort were the same as mine, I went along to get news of the Battalion. They proved to be a sergeant and a private of the "Royals", and the plane had come down in the Lowland Brigade area that morning. The captive, a pilot officer, was the only casualty in the ward. He was not badly hurt and was sitting up in bed with a bandage round his head.

One saw rather a forceful, square, tanned-looking face with strong features, very much like the usual sort of picture one always had of a Nazi German, although he disclosed that he was Austrian. The conversation I had with him was conducted with a curious absence of personal animosity, and even with good humour. He spoke no English but I knew some pidgin-German. I asked him when he thought Germany would win the war.

"This year, 1945," he said.

"Why?" I asked.

"Who do you think will win?" he countered.

"England," I said.

He grinned. "Oh, of course! But why?"

"Because we have more armies, an air force of thousands more planes than the Luftwaffe, and a great Navy which Germany is without," I said. "England, America and Russia are greater than Germany. How can you win?"

The answer came pat, with an assertive lift of the head, and for a moment he was like a small boy:

"Wir haben einen Fuhrer!"

I replied that we, too, had a leader. Churchill.

"Ah—Churchill!" he said. He made some remark about Churchill being no good, then said that as Churchill was good for England, so Hitler was good for Germany. "And Churchill is no good for Germany," I had to add. But he shook me:

"England is all right," he said.

He elaborated. . . .

England should be fighting with Germany, against Russia, and not with America. America was not good for England.

"Good," I said. "Germany is good; England is good. But why must they fight other people?" As for the Americans, they were our friends.

He left the question unanswered, but disbelieved America was our friend. He asked me why America had declared war on Germany. I said that if Germany had won, America would have been alone, with an enemy in the west in Germany, and in the east in Japan. So she had to enter the war.

To this he said Germany was no enemy of America.

It was a brick wall.

"You say Hitler is good for Germany," I said, "but how is that?" I waxed eloquent. In 1940 Germany was the strongest in Europe. Then Churchill our leader became, and Hitler did not send his soldiers to England and did not defeat us. He marched against Russia where thousands of Germans were killed and wounded, and the rest were being driven away again towards Germany. I reminded him of the sea, where all their best battleships, the *Graf Spee*, the *Bismarck*, and so on, had been sunk; and of our air force bombing the German homeland. I pointed to the German defeat in Africa: it had been "Kaput" in Africa.

But no.

He said I was talking propaganda. Hitler was still good. And he sat there in bed with his arms folded and his head held obstinately, not looking at me. Older than I, he laughed it all off, and turned to the escort and a Sister who had entered, who were interested spectators, and remarked with a nod towards me, "He speaks well! . . ."

But I was in the middle. I pressed on. There were the Germans in Italy: "Kaput." All the "friends" of Germany: Italy, Roumania and the others, "Alle Kaput." I came to my last point: Hitler had said that if the British ever landed in France we would be defeated in nine hours. But now our soldiers had come to Germany. "And you say Hitler is good?" I asked him.

He took me seriously again. Yes, Hitler is good because he will never surrender. "If Hitler goes, the Bolsheviks will come in."

I said that when Germany collapses the people will turn on Hitler and the Nazis.

He said that would not happen.

It was another brick wall.

He asked me why England had made war on Germany. Danzig was German, and he spoke quickly. I could not follow him.

I said that when Germany had defeated Poland we knew she would turn west, against Holland, Belgium, France and ourselves. My German limited me. I said Hitler did not wish England to be strong. Germany must be the strongest. All Europe must be under Germany. In all history Germany was war-like. There was 1914, 1870, Frederick the Great. . . . My German gave out.

His head was very obstinate. Everything was repeatedly denied. He got worked up. He said England had fought as many wars as Germany. He scoffed at the idea that Germany would have attacked us. He meant everything he said. It was still a brick wall.

"So," I replied, to finish, coming close to the bed, "when Germany is defeated, remember when I talked with you here."

He was excited, and like a small boy again. "And when

England is defeated, you remember when I talked with you here!" he almost shouted, turning on his elbow and pointing after me. With a despairing wave of the arm I withdrew.

Next morning I saw him being taken away on his journey to internment. He was dressed in his uniform and flying-jacket, and still had a bandage round his head. He said goodbye to his old escort, and at the end of the corridor, just before he disappeared, he caught sight of me. He turned for a moment to stare back at me as if he would have said something. But having just woken up, I stumbled on in the other direction to the washroom.

CHAPTER THIRTY

ONE MORE RIVER. . . .

IN 1918 Marshal Foch sounded his slogan: "Tout le monde
à la bataille!" But in 1944 General Eisenhower said that he
was "gonna throw a party on the Rhine"—and this was it.

Giant operations were necessary. The primary effort of the
Allied offensive into Germany was delivered north of the
Ruhr by the Northern Group of Armies of Field-Marshal
Montgomery; and up here, on one of the major mornings of
the Second World War, 8th February 1945, the decisive Battle
of the Rhineland was opened, by the fearful means of Operation
Veritable.

The thaw had set in, there were widespread floods and the
weather was vile.

Operation Veritable was carried out by the Canadian First
Army, reinforced with the whole offensive power of 21 Army
Group. The Canadians had a great reputation, and to many of
us from Second Army it came as a tribute to be fighting under
the army sign of the Maple Leaf.

All good things come to an end, and so, near Nijmegen, did
the Siegfried Line. Operation Veritable was launched from
Nijmegen on a devastatingly narrow front, and churned its
way in a south-easterly direction down the neck of land
widening out into the Rhineland between the Maas and the
Rhine. Four hundred and forty-six freight trains lifted a quarter
of a million tons of stores to the railheads for the battle. A
hundred miles of new roads had to be constructed and four
hundred miles of existing roads reconditioned. Half a million
air photographs and eight hundred thousand special maps were

issued. Thirty-five thousand vehicles took part, and five bridges had to be built across the Maas near Nijmegen, leading to the forward assembly areas.

The Veritable offensive lasted one month, and with its awful climax, Blockbuster, broke through the northern pivot of the main Siegfried defences around the forest called Reichswald, the Cleve-Goch switch system and the bitter belt of the Hochwald "lay-back", and ploughed through Xanten, heroic in the "Niebelungenlied" as the birthplace of Siegfried, to eliminate the last German resistance west of the Rhine. By the tenth day of the battle the enemy had committed eleven divisions, which included some of the best troops at that time surviving in the Wehrmacht.

On 8th February, First Canadian Army stood at just under half a million men, excluding still further reinforcements, for what we were told was to be the biggest single operation ever fought by British arms.

The Lowland Brigade started in the 15th Scottish divisional reserve. We had a new Brigadier, who had commanded the Blerick assault. One of those insouciant types who might have been born for war, and a descendant of Robert the Bruce; he was thirty-three. "The other two brigades are going to reach the Siegfried Line, and then our Brigade is going to go through the Siegfried Line," he had told each battalion, amid audible gasps. The "Blerick" recipe was to be used, and on the night of 7th-8th February, when the forward brigades were moving out to the assembly areas, we were concentrated in Nijmegen.

"A" Company were billeted in a school building. As we bedded down for rest, the night droned with hundreds of bombers going over to blast the Siegfried defences. Early on the morning of the 8th, for hour upon hour, the awful deep rumbling and shuddering of the opening barrage was the undertone to our troubled sleep.

For at last it was the Siegfried Line, and many of us felt a new fear. In its northern extension along the Netherlands frontier it was mainly earthworks, without the concrete fortifications of further south, and much was made of this fact. But it was still formidable—and there was more to it than this. The Rhine may have stood for the mystique of our enemies, but the Siegfried Line seemed their brute embodiment. The Rhine was symbolic, the Rhine was Victory, but the Siegfried barrier had a grimmer significance.

I woke in the small hours, in the bleak schoolroom at Nijmegen. A hurricane lamp was burning. Around, huddled in their blankets on the bare boards, were the officers of "A" Company. Our present Company Commander was a quiet-humoured regular from the Royal West Kents, and the fearful age of thirty-eight. There were also three young subalterns; one of them was awake, and I saw him there, on his back with his hands pressed intently together, his lips ceaselessly moving at his prayers. Outside the windows, the continuous massed thunder of the guns opening Veritable.

There was a huge cover-plan. Apparently guns were firing deceptive shoots along the entire British Front in Holland. The whole of the security and deception measures were so fabulous that only a couple of days beforehand our own reconnaissance parties had been allocated assembly areas along the Maas to the north of Breda and Tilburg, in ignorance of the fact that they were enacting a blind. By all manner of authentic bustle was it intimated to the enemy that the offensive was being launched into North Holland. For days there had been secret sandtable exercises on the real thing, down to battalion and company commanders, but only at the eleventh hour was the true destination divulged to the troops. While in the actual path of the assault was being fired the greatest artillery barrage of the Second World War.

A captured German soldier had written in a letter home which was found on him: "When Tommy began his attack he started with such a terrific artillery barrage that we lost leave of our senses."

And Operation Veritable was on.

The Corps of the Black Boar had been transferred bodily into the Canadian Army for the opening assault. Built up to a strength of over 200,000 men, it struck, under General Horrocks, on that grey, drizzly morning: the biggest army corps known to history. Five infantry divisions advanced on a six-mile front, behind the fire of 1400 guns.

If an analogy can be drawn between a plan of battle and some recognized sport, there is an instinctive quickening of comprehension in the mind of the British soldier, and it was so in the Black Boar Corps in Veritable. These divisions were as a line of forwards at football, the troops were told, which certainly brought us on to metaphorically familiar ground.

Attacking into the deeply flooded areas along the Rhine bank, where the river curved to Emmerich, were two Canadian divisions as outside and inside left. As centre forward, with the task of breaking through the Siegfried pivot called Nutterden, came the 15th Scottish. At inside right, to clear the Reichswald itself, were the Welsh Division. And at outside right, south of the Reichswald on the road to Goch, were the 51st Highland Division.

It was some team.

On the left the Canadians assaulted in amphibious vehicles and fought fantastic battles on "islands" among the floods. Dykes above Nijmegen were blown in an effort to drain the water, and millions of gallons poured through the breaches, but the enemy countered by blowing more dykes, and as much water came flooding in again. On the right, in the grim depths of the Reichswald, tanks crashed through the trees while others became bogged to their turrets in the heavy going. Further over, on the Highland Division front, hard fighting developed. In the centre the Lowland Brigade's "Blerick" on to Nutterden was supposed to follow through our forward brigades at 9pm the same evening, by artificial moonlight. But the weather was already playing havoc with the speed of the advance. Many aircraft were grounded, there was further rain, and all routes were mashed into an almost impassable condition.

The whole day we stayed bottled up in Nijmegen, with nerves keyed and tense bits of news flashing in from the battle. By 9pm the head of the Brigade had only begun to move off. We crossed the great Nijmegen bridge and thence were into a hellish night of being banged and jerked about in open Kangaroos in continual rain, crawling and stopping and getting stuck, and interminably lurching forward again. All night it went on. Our Kangaroo crews were Canadian, and there was a lugubrious glimmer of comic relief in the shape of a driver with "A" Company, a man with a black moustache and a long mournful face, in his overalls and tank beret, who revelled in being introduced to us as a "sad, sad baastard". The only item to distinguish one hour from the next came in pitch dark and a traffic jam a short way past the Dutch village of Groesbeek, with gun flashes flickering in the dripping night, when it percolated to us, soaked-through and cramped and half asleep, that we had crossed the frontier. We were on German soil.

A dank misty dawn saw the blurred armoured columns passing slowly through the shambles of Kranenburg village, captured the day before by 46 Highland Brigade. The land had risen a little now, and for the first time in months we were above sea-level. All around was the recent billeting area for German troops manning the forward Siegfried zone. In big white capitals the battered husks of buildings bore their slogans: "Wir glauben an Adolf Hitler!" read many, and on all sides the ubiquitous "Ein Volk! Ein Reich! Ein Fuhrer!" proclaimed itself. And as both the other battalions were still struggling up the quagmire axis some distance behind, our own Battalion, which had been leading in the order of march, were pushed on to take the Nutterden feature alone.

There was no halt. On top of twelve hours in the Kangaroos,

235

and twelve hours behind schedule, with all the cavalcade of supporting armour that was not bogged, we drove ahead. We were the first British Unit to breach the main belt of the Siegfried Line.

It was one of the great moments of the campaign. The mist had cleared and the rain was holding off for a while, though the sky was dull and overcast. We were passing over a sweeping belt of bare, gentle upland. Tactically it was mighty ground, reminding one much of the rolling land between Odon and Orne in Normandy. Various small hills or knolls, partly wooded, stood about; the chief of which, named Hingst-Berg, was by the hamlet of Nutterden that gave its name to the whole sector. Out to our right and slightly below us stretched the long dense edge of the Reichswald Forest, and Churchill tanks could be picked out, mud-green shapes clustered on the sombre dun earth, working level with the Welsh Division inside. Away to the left the landscape dipped into a grey haze; here the Canadians were battling through the low-lying inundations along the Rhine. There was not a single soldier on foot to be seen. The world was mechanized. Everything was going forward behind armour-plating on caterpillar tracks, and the air was filled with the noise of engines.

The actual Siegfried backbone was a minefield and a great anti-tank ditch, supported by a considerable chain of earthwork gun-emplacements and trenches; while the "defence overprint" maps cast their widespread skein of telltale information, from air photos and superimposed in blue, across the whole region from the frontier to Cleve. And straight over this hump of it forged our "Blerick", hindered by nothing more than long-range shelling.

Clearly the German infantry manning this belt had had the fight knocked out of them by the frightful barrage of 8th February, and the sight of us the next day was enough for most of them. Out they came from their trenches and bunkers around Nutterden to lay down their arms. Once over the anti-

236

tank ditch we "depouched" and advanced to our objectives, while whole bodies of enemy with their N.C.O.s in front, came doubling across the fields in perfect columns to give themselves up. Ten enemy officers were in the bag. Guns were overrun. A battalion headquarters was taken. The battalion commander and the commander of an artillery regiment were among the prisoners. There was little determined resistance, and at that sporadic, although "A" Company had a Kangaroo ambushed by bazookas, which resulted in all on board becoming casualties, and we also lost two platoon commanders. And at some stage in the proceedings the Regimental Sergeant-Major, who had fought at Dunkirk, ceremonially hoisted a quantity of washing.

The irrelevant memory remains of a solitary German woman—how she got there, goodness knows—at the height of the assault, hurrying along a track as fast as she could from danger. A middle-aged Frau in black, and the first enemy civilian one had seen. Beside her a British soldier, in full battle order, was carrying her suitcase.

But there was no break in the weather, and Veritable was still struggling for speed. The Welsh Division's axis had broken down, and their supplies had to be switched on to the 15th Scottish axis. Then the Black Boar Corps ordered the Wessex Division forward, to bypass Cleve and strike for Goch from the north, and up came their Kangaroo columns by the same Kranenburg axis, now glutted with the echelons of three divisions. Meanwhile, the hoped-for break-out of the Guards Armoured Division, mustered further back, was out of the question, while already the enemy were rushing a couple of parachute divisions, a Panzer Grenadier division and another Panzer division, into the Cleve and Reichswald region.

By 10th February five miles of the Nijmegen-Cleve road were under two feet of water. Soon the depth doubled, and for a period we could only be supplied by amphibious DUKWs and "Buffaloes". All other routes were giving way under the huge demands of the offensive, and the good road to Goch, south of the Reichswald, was strongly barred by the enemy.

To the south Montgomery's other pincer, the American Ninth Army, was held stationary by heavy flooding due to the enemy's control of the notorious Roer Dams. With the German reserves free to concentrate against the Canadian First Army, a more severe stage of the battle was being reached.

We were rushed forward from Nutterden, the afternoon we captured it, to seize the Matterborn feature above Cleve before our adversaries at Venlo, the 7th Parachute Division, got there. In all our armoured array again, with the Churchills, Crocodiles and Kangaroos, we advanced to contact in thunderous procession along the dipping, rising road to Cleve. "D" Company were in the van, with "A" Company next. An armoured scout-car overtook the column just before the move off, and standing in the turret a careless figure in dufflecoat and balmoral sailed by, with binoculars raised. It was the new Brigadier, disappearing into darkest Germany some way ahead of his leading troops, and immediately on his tail, its nose fairly buried into the stern of the scout-car for protection, followed a ludicrous jeep with its hood up. Inside the jeep, hunched over a map-board, a somewhat unhappy looking Brigade I.O. was darting apprehensive glances at the hostile horizons to either side.

Then to another scramble from the Kangaroos, and another attack. We were on the Matterborn high ground, key to Cleve, and occupied a straggling hamlet called Bresserberg. The impact was terrific. The defences were a double line of trenches and weapon pits, with a few pill-boxes. With a hideous din the tanks stood belting everything in sight with chattering Besas. Farm buildings and cottages, already wrecked by bombardment or bombing, smoked into flame at flying sprays of tracer. The bag of prisoners swelled, but we had made it with little time to spare, and advance parachutist elements were already being bumped as dusk was falling. Their trick was to shout "Wounded!" and wave a white flag, pretending to surrender, so that their comrades from a flank could ambush any of our men who went to bring them in, and as soon as we were wise to this the usual sanctity of a white flag was rudely depreciated.

So our first night in Germany came down on utter destruction and the crackling of fires. It is hard to reflect the violence of it. Always there was one more river and during these opening days of the Veritable offensive a wave of bitterness swept through the troops as never before. At last it was Germany: the thought never left you. Germany: it did not matter what damage we did.

German parachute formations were now arriving fast. Here or there you might see them through binoculars—perhaps a platoon of little grey figures working towards convenient ground behind a self-propelled gun. A brigade of the Wessex Division took a wrong turning among the confusion of tracks and found themselves in Cleve, where they were heavily attacked. The "Fusiliers" assaulted the wooded Clever-Berg. Our Battalion advance party, riding down into Cleve on tanks, was ambushed. A flight of German jet aircraft swooshed in and out of the clouds, making a circling Spitfire or two look like obsolete crates. We moved forward again, on foot, through dead parachutists under the trees at the Clever-Berg look-out tower. No rations were coming up and we were living on 24-hour one-man packs, as when we came to Normandy.

We entered Cleve. An old Baedeker will tell you that Cleve is "beautifully situated on the slopes of a wooded hill which at an early period formed the bank of the Rhine." It would point out the former ducal palace of the ancient Duchy, tell you about Henry VIII's fourth wife, the monument commemorating the legend of the Knight of the White Swan, and that Wagner's

"Lohengrin" was based on Cleve. But there was not much to remind one of these things when we got to Cleve. Seven hundred Lancasters had bombed it.

The defence overprint said "Built Up Area heavily Bombed and Cratered." That was from air photographs in January. Before the Lancaster raid.

The destruction recalled Falaise. Down the entire main street, at which bulldozers had already been at work, the engines of war of the British Army were packed nose to tail. There was havoc everywhere. Weary infantrymen dwelt in the cellars. These alone were practically unscathed, being reinforced and of enormous strength. The whole Rhineland had long been turned into a fortified zone.

Soon there was warning of the Panzer Lehr Division, while we were subjected to the worst shelling we had known for a long time, and by guns of big calibre. More of our own troops came trudging through. Somewhere ahead the cruel re-echoing of British Mediums could be heard bursting among enemy armour. A Canadian brigade relieved us, and big, magnificent specimens, they made a particular impression in this ruined wilderness.

We were pulled back into laager for two or three days on the former Bresserberg positions, now an ear-splitting "5.5" gun area, where we were held in readiness to support the Welsh Division on the edge of the Reichswald, in case of counter-attack. The appearance of a fresh enemy battle group, with tanks, duly threw all into a state of alert. Soon operational instructions were issued for the start of the assault southwards on Goch, which was to be an all-Scottish affair, with the Highland Division converging simultaneously from the west.

There was little dignity about Germany in defeat. They went down with raucous blare to the last.

Yet some there was. Left behind in the debris at Bresserberg were some little cards, presumably intended for distribution to the friends and relatives of a German soldier killed in battle, at some time, on some front, whose home had once been here. In heavy print they announced that "Hans Schmidt ist gefallen." The words lingered in one's mind. Before long one heard them again, listening-in to the gruff, abrupt radio announcement by Doenitz to the German people: "Der Führer ist gefallen. . . ." What a chord it struck; and with curious dignity, they had made the soldiers' wording serve.

And there were two enemy staff officers, complete with motorcar: we had captured them. One of them was reasonably solid and robust, but the other was not easily to be forgotten. He was dark, the face sensitive, and very German. Both were handled without ceremony and made to stand a long time with their hands up. He stood with his eyes roving apart, as a man does who holds on to his pride under great humiliation. He had fought for his country. Now he saw our planes in the sky and our tanks on the ground, and his country being ruined around him. The hurt was plain on his face. One of our sergeants in an ugly mood was soon at them, roughly searching them and stripping them of arms and papers. And the sergeant came to him, and tore the Iron Cross and ribbon from his tunic with all the rest. At this I took the Iron Cross from the sergeant, and gave it back to him. And in English, simply, he said: "Thank you."

CHAPTER THIRTY-ONE

END OF THE ROAD

WE were standing on the Clever-Berg somewhere near the watch tower; a small group of officers, staring ahead. Before us was the Rhineland. Away into the misty horizon stretched Germany. And in the middle distance, about five miles out, a wan silver streak glinted in the hazy plain.

In a few moments we moved on.

It was my first and only glimpse of the Rhine from Ben's Battalion.

Outside Battalion Headquarters there was only young Guy besides myself of the officers who had come through our every battle; and he was on U.K. leave during the opening of Veritable. At B.H.Q. there were only Giles the C.O., Hugh, Percy and Fred the Quartermaster who had come all the way; even Mac the Adjutant had gone to Division; even the Padre had left, to be Senior Chaplain. Others were less fortunate. Since June the Battalion had lost nearly sixty officers and had undergone 100 per cent turnover of their war establishment in casualties. The originals were a sprinkling, and at that frequently men who had been wounded and restored. "A" Company had seen six Company Commanders, and of the old 7 Platoon with whom I had landed in Normandy, but two men remained. The faces changed. Others filled the gaps.

I left them the day before the advance on Goch, to become an instructor at the Divisional battle-school in Belgium where the replacements were trained. Giles said he would recall me at the beginning of May. "You would be a fool not to go," said our Company Commander from the Royal West Kents. So I went.

The captain who relieved me as Second-in-Command "A" Company was wounded by a shell. The Company Commander from the Royal West Kents was killed in the woods beyond Goch. And from the watch tower at Cleve, Operation Veritable rolled away.

The remaining reserves were moved into the battle, now among the bitterest of the war. On 23rd February the American Ninth Army advanced across the Roer. On 26th February began the final phase, Blockbuster, to the Rhine. Later a fine reproduction appeared on the centre page of the *Illustrated London News*, signed by Brian de Grineau. Under his drawing the artist had written: "At 3.30am in a dense fog Goch defences were breached by Scottish infantry on Kangaroo armoured vehicles crashing into the town over a narrow causeway, improvised by a party of devoted Sappers, to bridge the anti-tank ditch guarding the northern approaches. . . ." But the commander of the men in the drawing had handed over to the next officer and turned back towards the Aid Post. He fell dead on the way. A machine-gun burst had struck him in the chest beforehand, when reconnoitring for the exploit, and so the last guest at our party by the Seine went out from the Battalion—for they were Ben's Battalion—in gay Gordon, originally of the anti-tanks. "Gallant" is an overworked word in wartime, but he was.

At the end of the month the Division were withdrawn to Belgium, reverting to Second Army for amphibious training.

"It was like being in the dressing-room at Murrayfield or Hampden before an international match." So the Lowland Brigade account describes the eve of the Rhine crossing. And on the night of 23rd-24th March the 15th Scottish went over. In amphibious "Buffaloes" between Xanten and Rees they crossed the great river, half a mile from bund to bund, the Highland Division in action on their left, the Commandos on their right, the bagpipes playing.

Individual enemy formations fought savagely, but twenty-four hours later our forces were out of their bridgeheads and the great rout began. Two hundred miles onward Ben's Battalion fought a neat battle at Uelzen town on the road to Hamburg, where Giles got a bar to his D.S.O. On 25th April, the American and Russian vanguards met on the central Elbe.

Before dawn, on the 29th April, the 15th Scottish with First Commando Brigade under command stormed the heights across the lower Elbe behind a vivid bombardment: to become the only division in 2 Army Group to have made assault crossings of all four major water obstacles—the Seine, the Escaut, the Rhine and the Elbe. It was the last operation; there were rumours that Himmler, surrounded by SS, was in command of the disintegrating enemy forces from a head-quarters some miles the other side of the river.

On 1st May, Doenitz announced Hitler's death to the German people on Hamburg Radio. Next day the British 6th Airborne Division contacted Russian spearheads at Wismar on the Baltic. On 4th May Keitel's emissaries surrendered to Field-Marshal Montgomery on Lüneberg Heath, and that night the message went out to our troops in Germany: "Germans surrendered unconditionally 1840 hours 4th May 1945. Hostilities on all Second fronts will cease at 0800 hours 5th May 1945."

A few days earlier I had been recalled to the Battalion, but orders had come through for the disbandment of the battle-school, and recalled personnel were to stay put in order to travel back as a body with the rest. The battle-school broke up on 7th May, and the staff and the last course of students travelled by train to the German frontier near the Reichswald, thence by commandeered Hamburg motorbuses over the long trek across Germany the way the Division had gone. The following night I was sitting in a farmhouse kitchen somewhere beyond Osnabrück, listening on a German wireless to the V.E. celebrations back in England. A picture of a young man in

Wehrmacht uniform was on the wall opposite me. The farmer and his wife were pottering around; I asked them when Germany would begin another war. They raised their eyebrows, demurring humbly. At midnight the war against Germany was formally ended.

A couple of nights later I was back in Ben's Battalion. I had wanted to be in at the finish, but just too late rejoined "A" Company.

They were still in their final operational area, between Hamburg and Lübeck, labouring under a monster anti-climax. Many had expected another summer, reducing fanatics in the southern redoubt. But Europe had collided into peace.

So ended their tale. Today you could follow the whole of it in a few days by motorcar, in less by train, by air in a few hours. But it was a long way to the boots that touched down on the Normandy sands. That plodded under the barrage past the broken little church tower at Norrey, into the deathly June corn; that crouched by the drumming churchyard at St Manvieu, with the whitened things glimmering through the rain and the dusk; stumbled up flickering paths with the "Nebelwerfers" dropping their giant cigarette-stubs on Hill 113; that trod over the fallen boys in the Bois de l'Homme, and stole down the hedgerows at Estry. To the boots that swept through the miles of cheers and handgrips, through tumult and "Tipperary", and a Flemish carillon ringing the "Road to the Isles", and clattered into the bridgehead at Aart. Arnhem; and the boots that went into the dank Netherlands. The clusters of dead paratroops, and the dull names, Donderdonk, Liemde and Boschkant, lurking beyond the dripping woods, and the road being cut, and the outrun Army. To the boots racing from night firesides at Tilburg; slithering over the peatlands at Meijel; boots awkwardly stilled on the antennae of "S" mines; grey boots protruding on stretchers; boots smashing into Blerick-Venlo. Boots treading weeks of debris and shattered glass. Boots out of Nijmegen into the crater-peppered Rhineland; the boots of the men who went into Goch, and over the Rhine, to the end of the road.

Some remain in the Fields they won. . . . The others, I suppose, are ordinary human beings again.